Million Dollar Projects
from the 5 & 10¢ Store

Also by Leslie Linsley

Million Dollar Projects
from the
5 & 10¢ Store

Leslie Linsley

Design and photography by Jon Aron

St. Martin's Press • New York

Marek

Photograph on page 146 courtesy of Ladies Home Journal; photographer Bruce Wolfe. Photographs on page 153 courtesy of The Borden Company.

Library of Congress Cataloging in Publication Data

Linsley, Leslie.
  Million dollar projects from the five and ten cent store.
  1. Handicraft.   I. Aron, Jon.   II. Title.
TT157.L4847   745.5   81-21441
ISBN 0-312-53249-0   AACR2

Printed in the United States of America

Contents

The first 5 & 10¢ store opened by F. W. Woolworth, June 21, 1879, at Lancaster, Pa.

Introduction

In the year 1878 the first five and ten cent store was opened in Lancaster, Pennsylvania. It was a uniquely Yankee invention that would become a multi-billion dollar business with more stores than any chain in the world. The name "Woolworth's" would become instantly recognizable to countless millions around the world and the words "Woolworth's" and "Five and Ten" would be synonymous. Over the years Americans would sing, "I found a million dollar baby in a five and ten cent store," and "Diamond bracelets Woolworth's doesn't sell baby." Today Woolworth's does indeed sell diamonds in some of its European stores, but it's harder and harder to find anything for a nickel or a dime.

The five and ten has changed a lot since Frank Winfield Woolworth opened that first store. Now it's often referred to as the variety or novelty store and carries everything from underwear to appliances. People aren't even sure if it's still referred to as a five and ten. But in almost every town and city in this country there still remains some version of the old-fashioned five and ten where we know we'll find whatever it is we're looking for at a price that isn't alarming. Even in New York City with all the spectacular department stores and elegant boutiques, we still find a Lamston's or a Woolworth's in every section of town.

And while all the fancy merchandise has been added, the same basic aisles remain, reassuringly predictable, in every five and ten in the world.

All of us have grown up with the familiarity of the five and ten. The appearance inside may have changed with the times, but the allure of a five and ten is still there. The five and ten satisfies our needs on many levels. It is here that we find the endless cards of sewing notions, school supplies, paper goods, hardware, holiday decorations and all the fixings for art-and-craft projects. Our creative impulses come out in the five and ten.

The five and ten brings back feelings of nostalgia. This is the place that provided endless hours of fascination. There were always surprises to be found and while there is little to buy for five or ten cents it is still the only place we can really stretch a dollar.

The dime store is also the place where many young children committed an innocent childhood crime. How tempting were all those goodies just lying there to be admired, fondled, and daringly pocketed. Oh the excitement of all those loose little things right out where one could touch them.

The original idea to make merchandise accessible was conceived over a hundred years ago when F.W. Woolworth first set up his "5 cent counter" on a ten-foot long improvised stand. Here he openly displayed the staples of the Yankee peddler: safety pins, thimbles, combs, collar buttons, buttonhooks, boot straps, pencils, dippers, and harmonicas. There were items that were hard to move until they were displayed under the homemade sign reading, "Any Article on This Counter Five Cents."

On that first opening day 2,553 nickel purchases had been made and by the next summer the "Great Five Cent Store" as it was called was changed to "5 and 10 Cent Store" and finally to "Woolworth's 5 and 10 Store." The famous red-front stores with the diamond W trademark lasted until 1968 when it was phased out by the modern blue logotype. However, in some old sections of a town you can still find a red sign that reads, "F.W. Woolworth Co. 5 and 10 Store."

When I decided to write a book that would present projects made with materials exclusively from the five and ten it occurred to me that perhaps attitudes had changed. Did people still call it a five and ten? Did they still go to the five and ten before shopping elsewhere or had they forgotten what was there and that they could still get a bargain? Had the quality of the items held up in comparison to those found in competitive stores? Did they still think of the five and ten as a practical place to find something? Did they still think of it as one-stop shopping and was there any nostalgia left in regard to the dime store? I went to see an executive of the F.W. Woolworth Co. for some answers.

The Woolworth Building is located in lower Manhattan across from New York's City Hall. It was built in 1913 and at the time of its construction was the tallest building in the world. To this day it is regarded as one of the most majestic buildings in the city although it is now only the 14th tallest in the world.

We met in one of the large offices housed in the cathedral-like building that Frank Woolworth built with his own money. His portrait loomed above. Somehow, in this environment, I felt miles away from any five and ten cent surroundings.

But as I asked my questions and listened to the stories about how the five and ten came into being, the romance of a store filled with thousands of goodies came to life. I learned that while Woolworth now operates retail units under a variety of trade names there are still 4,416 Woolworth five and tens in all fifty states and Europe.

While the merchandise varies throughout the country you can be sure to find the same basic inventory from one store to the next.

Five and ten cent stores are responsive to changes in the country, but, by and large they still serve the same purpose, which is to provide us with those little items that solve everyday problems to make life easier. Every five and ten is divided into sections that include familiar things that everyone needs at one time or another. Often we find something we weren't even looking for.

As a craft designer and writer for almost twenty years, I've spent many hours in five and tens. I go there for materials and inspiration. Before buying anything I look for it first in the five and ten. I am familiar with five and tens from Florida to Connecticut and have been overwhelmed by the enormous amount of staples and the variety carried by the individual stores. I've toured the country promoting my books and while traveling have checked out five and tens in St. Paul, Los Angeles, San Francisco, Chicago, Texas and Atlanta and I am never disappointed. It's a creative adventure and the mixed bag of products, often bought on impulse, results in the most spontaneous creations.

As we move into a new decade, crafts, along with our style of dress and home accessories are taking a new turn. We don't have the same kind of spare time that we used to have and we care more about the quality of our time at home. After a brief decline in popularity, crafts are again on the rise. According to a recent survey of craft and hobby manufacturers, in this cost-conscious era the increase in sales has been substantial.

However, the new resurgence of craft activity is different than in the past. No more expensive looms or special equipment, no courses that take months to learn the craft. Now people are concentrating on adapting traditional crafting techniques and skills for quick and easy-to-make but good-looking projects. Without compromising one's design standards, craft projects that are made with less time and effort offer the enjoyment of making gifts and home accessories without a total commitment to the craft or to an extended period of time.

The new weekend home crafter is the same person who used to spend months working on a needlepoint pillow when crafting was a way of filling one's time. Now she or he prefers to use those skills on smaller, less time-consuming projects that offer the same good-looking results. Due to exposure, we've become more sophisticated in our tastes and demand better design in all areas. And this is true of everyone regardless of economic, educational, or social background.

I started my crafting career designing products that were sold in New York boutiques and department stores. All my ideas did not come about while sitting in a studio. I was exposed to and looking for new ideas all the time. Sometimes my designs resulted from suggestions made to me by the buyers I sold to, and when my work began to appear in magazines I received the invaluable feedback that comes from that kind of exposure.

The prices I received for my work had nothing to do with the cost of materials, but rather the design ideas and the craftsmanship that went into the technique of applying those designs. My experience has shown me that often the simplest, most elegantly designed project is one that is the easiest to make with common, ordinary materials.

Take a good look at all those handsome extraordinarily beautiful boutique items that you admire and that are so handsomely priced and you'll realize that the materials can be found in the five and ten. This is not to minimize a clever idea, a well-designed or expertly crafted project. However, if you accept this first aspect, that price is not always related to the cost of materials, you'll see how you can, with some instructions, afford to make what you admire.

The projects in the book have the flavor of what is currently stylish. Every ingredient that has gone into making them is available in the five and ten, often an alternative material for a more costly product. An example of this can be found in the project on page 78. I spotted this item in an expensive jewelry store and stood looking at it long enough to figure out how to make a reasonable facsimile. Try it yourself. Don't look at the list of materials, but study the picture long enough to figure out what elements could be used to achieve the same effect.

Approach the five and ten with the purpose of collecting ideas. Don't have any objective. Walk around and see what two elements you can put together. Take a chance for 69¢, take something home. See what you can come up with from a piece of felt for 19¢. Go into sections of the five and ten you don't usually go into. Try to imagine it's your first time in the store. The range of items is much broader than you'd imagine because most people confine themselves to those areas that have what they're looking for.

Five and tens respond to the change of seasons, special events, and holidays with specific items that are only carried at those times. It's easy therefore to be prepared to buy artificial chrysanthemums, orange and black construction paper, and colorful back-to-school book covers in the fall when there is a good stock. At Christmastime stock up on the items that are gone after the season and collect your heart designs on paper, stickers, paper plates, and napkins during the month of February. It's hard to get these items at any other time.

During Easter take advantage of the pastel colors, artificial spring flowers, egg-dyeing kits, and plastic straw baskets. In the summer you can get all the picnic items and brightly colored paper goods. Baskets and flower pots take up more space on the shelves in the spring and summer months. Utilize the colors, items, designs, and styles of the current theme be it Christmas, summer, back to school, gardening, Halloween, Fourth of July, or Valentine's Day.

When Frank Woolworth added ten cent goods to the line it enabled him to scout bargains from many more manufacturers. One such item was the Christmas tree ornaments that he popularized in America. This became a precedent for buying new and never before mass-merchandised items that are still seasonally introduced to the stores.

Every season designers in all fields offer something new to consider. And with every decade we are faced with more information, more products, and more needs to contend with. As a result our tastes are constantly changing. All these factors have an effect on how we spend our money. And since we see more than we can afford, we have to do without much of it. In every area of fashion, be it clothing, jewelry, furniture, gifts, or accessories, we can find a cheaper version that is similar to the more expensive original.

But often the cheaper version doesn't satisfy us. One way to have something better that is affordable is to make it. Certainly in an age when everything is manufactured it has become extremely difficult to find anything handmade and then at a reasonable price. In the not-too-distant future a handmade item may be a rarity.

The people who are making things today are valuing them more. Families are using Christmas as a reason to make ornaments that can become keepsakes. If they could afford to buy these things they would not be as valuable.

With the price of homes and home furnishings rising, people are making whatever accessories they can in order to have them. When you see how easy and inexpensive it is to cover a lampshade with your own fabric, for example, you

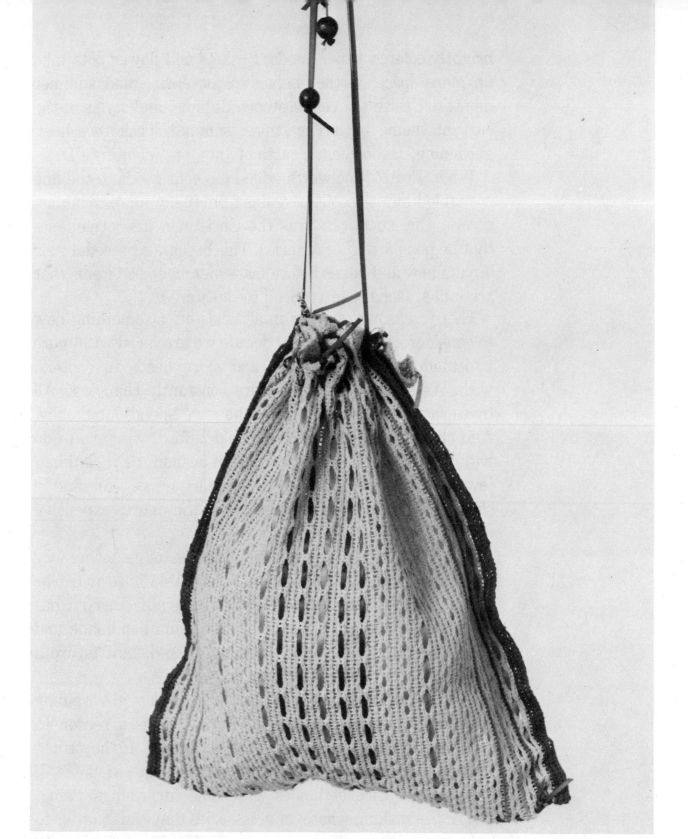

Weave ribbon through 2 dishcloths for a tote.

won't want to settle for a cheap store-bought substitute. Picture frames that add up to big dollars can be custom made for a fraction of the cost. And those boutique T-shirts that cost under $5 to make, and sell for $35 and more, are easier to create than you'd think. Pillows, an age-old decorating accessory, are outrageously priced, especially if the fabric is decent. The foam pillows in the five and ten are not exactly plush, but they sell for under $3 so you can detract from the negative aspect with terrific fabric.

And there is always a cheap version of the cheap version for a lot of home furnishings. Take lamps for example. When the clip-on studio lamps came into vogue there were inexpensive versions of the originals found in better art supply and department stores. The five and ten also carried its version for half to a third the price.

The famous Parson's table is still the most popularly copied design found in unfinished furniture shops. And the five and ten has its version. It's a bit smaller and made of plastic rather than wood, but taken for what it is—the best outdoor table to be found for the price—it's still a good buy.

If we appreciate nice things then we want to continue to add to that enjoyment. It's hard to make compromises, but we surely can't have everything. To cut back due to the rising costs of living, many people by necessity have been looking for alternative ways to have what they want. The contradiction of art-and-craft sales increasing in a tight economy doesn't seem so preposterous. It makes sense to put your money, time, and effort into that which will reap the most rewards. We end up with good feelings about being responsible, figuring out how to have extras for less money and, of course, the satisfaction of having made it can't be minimized.

The following projects are simple to create and most of them cost under $6 to make. If the item costs more than $3 or $4, and art supplies were needed to transform it, I weighed the decision carefully. Was it worth more for what I would end up with? Sometimes it worked out, other times I eliminated a good idea because in my estimation it wasn't worth the overall cost.

We all value our time. For the most part the projects are accessories rather than necessities. The premise of this book is that no such project should take more time than it's worth. I had to evaluate each project by this criterion as well. If it took more than a couple of hours it had to be an exceptionally good idea to be included. Many of the projects are so simple that only the briefest directions are needed. I think these were often the best. My favorite is the plant holder on page 120. I was passing a Woolworth's and saw the straw hat in the window. It didn't take two seconds to visualize it as a plant holder so I went in and bought it without another thought.

Some of the projects were on-the-spot inspirations, some were given a lot of time to think through the design and construction, some resulted in response to a good idea that I thought could work out. The patterns, designs, and dimensions were often reworked several times until the right style was achieved. Many of the projects are copies of expensive items that I saw in boutiques and department stores. The ribbon belts on page 98 are an example of this. Here is a good idea that was easy to copy for exactly one-third the retail price. The time to create it is minimal, as the materials and construction have been figured out for you.

A great many of the projects came about as a result of bringing home odds and ends from the five and ten. Most of them were unrelated items that seemed to have potential. They were either obviously useful, well proportioned, nicely colored, interesting material, or a good buy. An example of one such item is the toothbrush and toothpaste traveling case (page 128). Aside from being a good size to hold pencils I found them in unusual colors not often used for these items. Inexpensive artificial flowers are not usually exciting, but when I found them in the new dusty pastels I felt they had some potential.

Clay flower pots afforded another area for inexpensive, good design. The pots are well proportioned, a beautiful terra-cotta, and they inspired simple, elegant decorations. If you saw them in a gift shop you would not be shocked if they were priced at four times their cost.

Another offering of the five and ten cent store that intrigued me was containers. Everything comes in a container. If you go through the entire five and ten just looking at packaging you'll find a wealth of containers to transform. For example, a Q-Tip box has a sliding drawer. Imagine covering the box with Con-Tact or wrapping paper, add a bead for a drawer pull and you have a little jewelry box. Stack several and wrap them together and you have a very inexpensive desk organizer.

Sucrets and candy tins make elegant pill boxes when decorated (see page 114) and the variety of plastic containers is endless.

When you go to throw out a can, box, tin, or tube, think first if it has possibilities. A little ribbon, some fabric or paint can make something beautiful and useful out of a throwaway.

The notions department can yield all kinds of plastic boxes such as those used to hold pins and needles. Bobby pin or Band-Aid boxes are good for travel size sewing kits or button holders (see pages 108 and 110).

Clothing is an entire section often overlooked. We think of the five and ten cent clothing as cheap in every sense. This is not entirely true. The selection of cotton underwear carries the name brand of those found in better department stores and very often odd lots of expensive items are bought up and sold for unbelievable bargains. T-shirts can be the basis for all kinds of creative expression and quite frankly the cheaper ones often fit better. Regular white ankle socks sell for around a dollar. If you buy them in beautiful pastel colors in a clothing store they will cost at least five dollars. If they have any decoration on them you will pay six to ten dollars. Nothing could be simpler than dyeing and decorating socks and for five dollars you can have four pairs each with a different design.

Jewelry is another area I had some fun with. Fortunately costume jewelry is popular right now and almost anything goes. In fact the more outrageous the better. Nowhere can you find more inspiration, more things to combine in this area than in the five and ten. Try the hardware and housewares sections and then move on to school supplies, relating everything you see to possible jewelry ideas.

There are of course just plain good buys that don't relate in any way to a project or makeover. And they aren't cheaper versions of better ideas. They include such items as plants, dishtowels, coat hangers, plastic sweater boxes and other closet organizers, lightswitch plates, window shades, paper and party supplies, to name a few.

Just as it was in the early 1900s the five and ten today still offers the widest range of value we can find anywhere. At the time of Frank Woolworth's death in 1919 the F.W. Woolworth Co. boasted sales of over $100 million. Almost all of the 22 million families in the United States browsed and bought things for nickels and dimes. During that year the stores sold 10 million packages of chewing gum, 26,000 tons of candy, 100 million postcards, and 15 million bars of soap. Six hundred thousand babies wore 10 cent gold-filled rings from Woolworth's. It was then, as it is now, the greatest bazaar in America.

Boutique designs for a fraction of the price

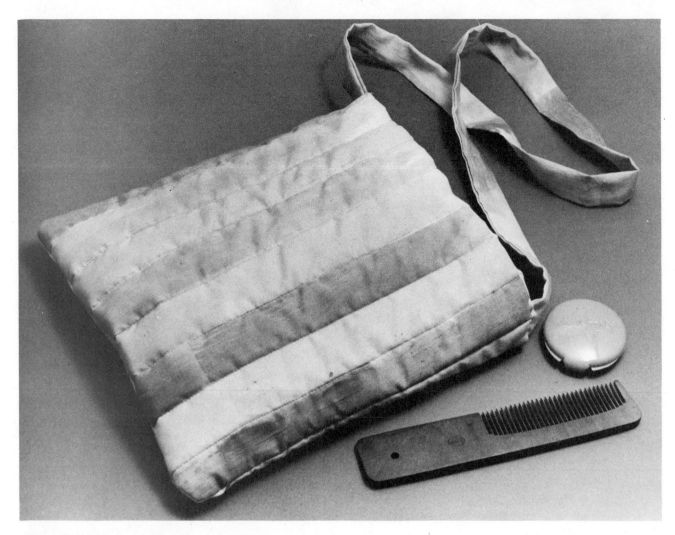

Quilted pastel purse

Fabric crayons are used here to create a rainbow of beautiful soft pastel colors on ordinary cotton muslin or polyester. The purse measures a convenient 10 × 10 inches and is a good everyday size. However, you can make a smaller one for cosmetics and a larger size as a carry-all. This one utilizes six colors. If you make a purse to go with a specific outfit, combine those colors that match.

Materials: 1 yard of white cotton fabric, scissors, pins, pencil, ruler, 2 pieces of polyester batting 10 × 10 inches each, 1 package Crayola Craft Fabric Crayons (toys or notions), newspaper, white Bond paper, iron.

Directions: Cut four pieces of fabric 10½ inches square. Cut one strip of fabric 2¼ × 36 inches long.

Rule off the Bond paper into 1½ inch strips. Place the paper on newspaper and color each strip with a different crayon color. Alternate light and dark colors for the best effect. Cut each strip apart.

Pad the ironing board with newspaper and place one piece of fabric on top. Put the first crayon strip face down along one side of the fabric. Set the iron for cotton. When hot, press down on the back of the crayoned paper for 3 to 5 seconds, then remove the iron. Lift the strip of

paper. The color will be transferred to the material. If it is too faint, recolor and repeat. Continue to apply each strip of color in this way until the fabric is covered. Make more strips of colored paper as needed. Do the same for the back piece of the purse.

Rule off strips of paper 2½ inches wide until you have enough for the handle strap of the purse. Do freehand coloring, changing crayons every 2 inches or so, with one color running right into the next. Transfer the color to the long strip of fabric.

With right side of fabric together stitch across the top edge. Repeat with the back pieces. Turn and press. Insert a piece of polyester batting between each set of fabric and pin at the sides. Quilt each piece by stitching between each strip of color.

With right sides together pin front and back quilted fabric pieces at the sides and bottom. Stitch together. Trim close to seamline and turn right side out.

With right sides together fold the long strip in half lengthwise and press. Stitch down the long edge. Attach a safety pin to one end and turn right side out by threading closed pin through the strip. Stitch to the inside at each side of the purse.

Ring pillow sachet

This delicate ring or sachet pillow is made from a very full-boarded lace handkerchief. It cost $1.39 to make. The decorative appliqués can also be purchased for approximately fifty cents to a dollar. This is a good project for hand embroidery since the area is small and calls for a delicate design. When filled with sweet smelling potpourri or a dab of perfume on the polyester filling you have an elegant but easy-to-make shower gift.

Materials: 1 lacy handkerchief, small piece of white cotton fabric for back, embroidered appliqués, 1 yard of ¼ inch pink satin ribbon, needle, thread, scissors, polyester fill.

Directions: Cut a square of cotton ½ inch larger than the plain area of the hanky. Turn the edges in ½ inch all around and press. Stitch this piece to the back of the handkerchief on three sides. Fill generously with polyester fill and slip stitch open side.

Stitch the ribbon around the hanky at the inside edge of the lace border. Add the appliqués with hand stitching where they look best. Some handkerchiefs are pre-embroidered. If you use them you may want to add a full lace border if none exists.

Basket of cheer

Find a plain little inexpensive basket, paint it, fill it with greens or candy canes and you have a delightful last-minute Christmas gift. If you make several you can line them up on a window sill or mantelpiece and place a small gift in each. Use these instead of the traditional stockings. Cluster them together in the middle of your table, fill each with dried flowers or small plants and you have an original centerpiece. Any way you use them these simply painted baskets will look sensational.

Materials: tight-weave basket, white spray paint, green and red acrylic paint, small artist's brush.

Directions: Spray paint the entire basket inside and out, let dry and paint again. It is difficult to paint a perfect design over a bumpy surface, therefore the simpler the design the better. Here we have a stem, two leaves and a berry all done with a dab or a dot of the paint brush. Begin by marking the basket with a pencil so that each design will be evenly spaced. No two are exactly alike which gives this project a charming style.

Desk set

Here is a familiar object that's better looking than we usually expect this item to be. It's a good gift to make because it's useful and perhaps something we don't buy for ourselves.

Paper boutiques sell paper-covered pencil sets that are easy to make in spare time. The assortment of wrapping paper is sometimes limited in the five and ten but a small overall design in a bright color suitable for this project shouldn't be difficult to find. Con-Tact paper can also be used and you'll be surprised at the current selection. Some of the designs are fairly contemporary now that its use is not relegated exclusively to kitchen drawers.

Materials: ¼ yard of Con-Tact or 1 package of wrapping paper, piece of poster board (school supplies or art section), tape, white glue, ruler, scissors, spray varnish (optional).

Directions: Cut 4 pieces of cardboard 2 × 4 inches. Cut 1 piece 2 × 2 inches. Tape the four sides together and tape the square to the bottom to create the open top box.

Cut a rectangle of paper 8¼ × 4½ inches. Cut another piece 2 × 2 inches. Coat the back of the larger piece with glue and wrap it around all four sides of the box. Overlap the paper slightly on the bottom and the top edge. Coat the smaller piece with glue and cover the bottom with paper. If you'd like a shiny finish on the box give it a coat of spray varnish or clear nail polish.

Cut strips of paper wide enough to wrap each pencil. Coat the back of each strip with glue and roll the paper around each pencil.

Decoupage vase

Inexpensive ceramic jars can be made to look like expensive earthenware with the right decoration. Look for one in an earth tone that can be enhanced with an outdoor scene. Or, you might find one in jet black or cherry red and apply an Oriental design. The designs are cut from greeting cards or wrapping paper.

The technique of decoupage is usually time-consuming but in this case much of the tedious work has been eliminated. Because the ceramic surface is smooth no sanding or painting is necessary and if a simple design is used the cutting is quite easy.

Materials: ceramic cup, jar .or mug; glue; clear spray varnish; small scissors; sponge.

Directions: Select a paper design that will fit the area of your vase. Cut out the design and spread the back with glue. Position each piece on the vase and press with a damp sponge. This will remove all excess glue that oozes from the edges. Let dry.

To protect the paper design coat with clear spray varnish. Let this dry and repeat two or three times.

Gift soap

An ordinary bar of soap is decorated with decals and self-sticking hearts. This is an instant decorating idea. Use it in the bathroom when guests come. Insert it with a gift of lingerie or towels or bring it with you as a house gift. Remember that around Valentine's Day it's easy to find the stickers, cupid decals, and doilies shaped like hearts (good for placing under the soap in a gift box), but at other times of the year you may not find them easily. Choose the designs according to what's available. Seals and decals of

flowers, birds, leaves, and butterflies are sold throughout the year. But take advantage of seasonal items; for example, Christmas package stickers will decorate soap that can be used as stocking stuffers.

The scrollwork on the Sweetheart soap shown here is emphasized with gold acrylic paint which is applied with a pointed artist's brush. Once the stickers and decals are in place, coat the top of the soap with clear nail polish. The soap can be used down to the last sliver.

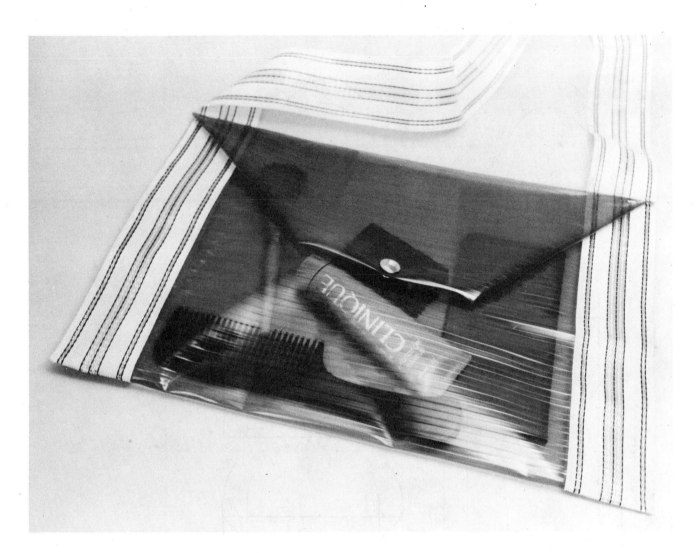

See-through portfolio

All-purpose transparent ribbed vinyl is sold on rolls by the yard. It is used for such purposes as foul-weather protection over carpeted doorway areas or to cover car floors. It is flexible, sturdy, and comes in appealing colors like shocking pink, lavender, red, blue, as well as clear. It is easy to work with and can be sewn on a machine using heavy-duty thread. This large-size carry-all is waterproof and good looking.

Materials: ¾ yard vinyl, 1 package plastic lounge chair repair webbing (garden supplies), heavy duty thread, one snap (notions), scissors.

Directions: Cut a piece of vinyl 16 × 27 inches. Cut a piece of webbing 2 yards long. Turn one raw end of webbing down and pin 20 inches of the webbing down one side edge of the vinyl. Stitch together across the folded end and down the outside and inside edge.

Fold the other raw end of the webbing under and bring it around the vinyl and attach the last 20 inches to the corresponding side of the vinyl. Reinforce with stitching at points indicated on the diagram.

Fold up 10 inches of web-edged vinyl with wrong sides together and pin along the outside edges. Stitch the front and back together along 10 inches.

Make an envelope fold of the remaining flap of

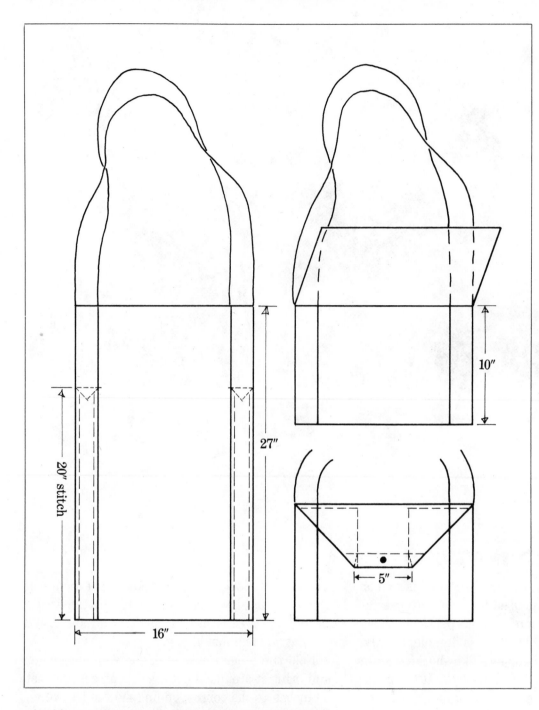

vinyl by turning down each corner (see diagram). Secure with a pin. The top of the flap will be 5 inches across. Turn the top raw edge down ½ inch and pin.

Stitch along the outside edge of the vinyl flap. Find the center of the outside flap and attach a decorative snap as per directions on the package.

Mushroom apron

This is not only an adorable apron for a child to wear but it is also practical. It's made from oilcloth and clear storm window vinyl covering found on large rolls in the section where Con-Tact is sold. Purchased by the yard this material is often used to cover an outdoor picnic table. The mushroom spots are Dennison self-adhesive stickers (school section).

Materials: ½ yard of red vinyl or oilcloth, ½ yard of clear vinyl plastic, ½ yard of white cotton fabric, 1 package of ¾ inch stickers, 1½ yards of ¾ inch cloth ribbon braid or cording for ties.

Directions: Enlarge pattern and cut one piece of red vinyl to measure 19 inches across the bottom and 10 inches high at the center of the curve.

Cut a piece of clear vinyl and a matching piece of white cotton for the base. It will be 11½ × 12½ inches with a slight curve at the bottom.

Turn the side and bottom edges of the cotton piece ¼ inch to the back and press. Place the clear vinyl over the front of the cotton and stitch around three edges (excluding the top).

Center the top edge of the base on the bottom edge of the top with right sides together. Stitch across creating a ½ inch seam.

Cut three 18 inch lengths of ribbon. Stitch one to the back of each side of the mushroom top for tying. Stitch each end of the other ribbon to the top of the apron with 7 inches between. This ribbon will go over the head. You may want to adjust the length on your child before stitching it to the apron.

The last step is one your child can do alone or with you. Place sticker dots over the top two thirds of the mushroom bib, spacing them at random until you feel they look good. If you don't like the first arrangement, they peel away easily for replacement.

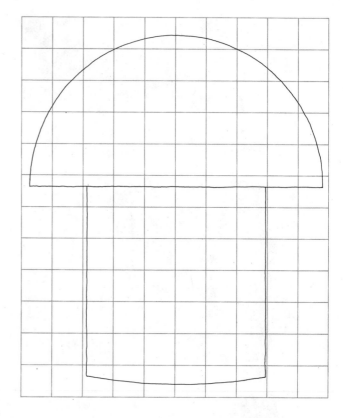

Each square equals 1″

A child's purse

The simple shape of a mushroom is always appealing and mushroom designs have surfaced on everything. We find toadstool salt-and-pepper shakers, candle holders, pin cushions and even lamps. This little felt purse is easy to make and fun to wear. You can be true to the mushroom colors of brown and white or be imaginative with bright yellow, red, or orange. The felt pieces are 9 × 12 inches.

Materials: 1 piece of white felt, 1 piece of brown felt, white glue, scissors, 1 yard cloth seam binding or ribbon for shoulder strap, small square of Velcro.

Directions: Cut two pieces of white felt for the base using the pattern provided here. Cut two pieces of brown for the top. Cut five white circles.

Sew one brown top to one white base with the edge of the brown overlapping the top edge of the white. Repeat for the back pieces.

Pin front and back together and stitch around outside edges leaving 6 inches open at the top. Insert either ends of the ribbon or seam binding between the brown felt on either side of the opening. Tack securely.

Apply a small amount of white glue to one side of the circles and press down onto the top of one side of the mushroom. See project for placement.

Attach a small piece of Velcro to either side of the opening on the inside. This will allow the user to close and open the purse easily.

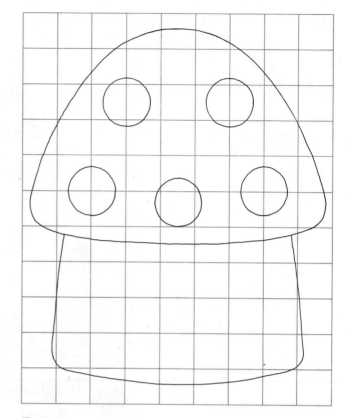

Each square equals 1"

36

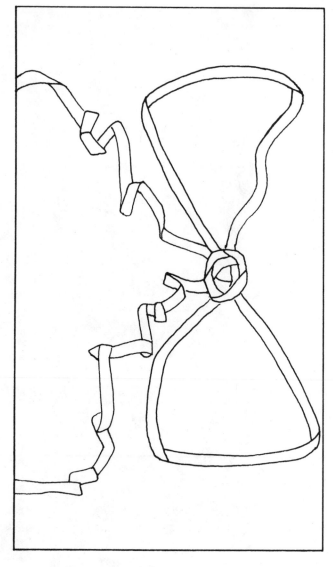

Beaded shirt

A plain white cotton undershirt costs about $3. Add a satin ribbon bow and some tiny pearl beads and you will find it for $30 in most boutiques. This is only one way to turn an undershirt into an outershirt so use the notions department to get some ideas for trimmings.

Materials: 1 undershirt, 1 package blue ⅛ inch satin ribbon (made by Offray), 1 package tiny pink beads, thin sharp needle, thread, scissors, tracing paper.

Directions: Trace the bow provided here and place the tracing in position inside the shirt. Hold the garment against a window pane and trace the outline in pencil. Use this as a guide for placing the ribbon.

Pin the ribbon to the shirt front and stitch by hand. Add clusters of beads by sewing them to the shirt with a fine needle. You can also add an embroidered appliqué to the center of the bow. You will find small rose buds and other delicate pastel flowers which can be used with this design.

If you want to make these shirts more unusual, they can be dyed with Rit fabric dye before decorating.

Quilted place mat

Pastel place mats look especially pretty in the summer. Or brighten up a breakfast area any time of the year with this loose crayon design. Projects done with this technique always turn out well because the colors are so appealing. The crayons will appear to be harsher than they become when transferred to the fabric. It's a deceptively easy technique and the results are quite professional looking.

Material: 2 pieces of cotton fabric 11½ × 17½ inches, 1 piece of polyester batting slightly smaller, 1 package of fabric crayons, 3 sheets of white Bond paper, newspaper, ruler, pencil, iron, scissors, and pins.

Directions: Rule off Bond paper into 1½ inch wide rows. Color each strip with a different crayon. Cut the strips apart and then in half.

Turn the raw edges of each piece of fabric under ¼ inch all around and press. Pad your ironing board with newspaper and place both fabric pieces face up on top.

Heat the iron to cotton setting. Place one strip of paper with the color side down on one corner of the fabric. Press the hot iron over it for 3 to 5 seconds and remove. Lift the strip and place it down at random. Heat again. Repeat. Each time you do this the color will get fainter. Place another color strip next to the first and heat. Repeat as before. As the fabric begins to fill up with color you can put one color over another. You will be creating an abstract pattern of overlapping colors with varying degrees of intensity.

Place the batting between the two fabric pieces and stitch around all four edges. Stitch along the lines between the colors to quilt the place mat.

Decorative combs

Gather all your ribbons, yarn, buttons, sequins, feathers and any other odds and ends you can find to decorate a bunch of combs and barrettes.

If you haven't noticed, hair combs and barrettes have been turning up everywhere and they are gorgeous. Some are simply adorned by wrapping the top with colorful yarn, others are elaborately fashioned with feathers, silk flowers, glass beads, and more. The prices can go as high as ten dollars for a single comb but you can make your own for a fraction of this cost.

Use white glue to attach your elements.

Materials: ¼ inch satin ribbon, buttons, paper seal, artificial flowers, yarn, embroidery thread, embroidered appliqués.

Ribbon comb

Leave 4 to 5 inches of ¼ inch ribbon hanging at one side and begin to wrap the ribbon around the top until the comb is completely covered. Continue wrapping as you bring the ribbon back to the starting point.

Tie the two ribbon ends and leave another 4 to 5 inches hanging so you have both ends hanging down on one side.

Cut off the excess ribbon. Thread a white button on the end of each ribbon and leave loose. Attach a decal or paper seal to the front on the opposite side of the comb.

Artificial flowers

Wrap the top of the comb with green pearlized embroidery floss. Leave a few inches at the end.

Take apart one stalk of artificial flowers and glue the flower to one side of the comb on top of the floss.

Thread the long end of the floss through the center of another flower and make a knot in the center of the flower to secure it. This flower will hang loose.

Feather butterfly

You can create a butterfly by gluing feathers to the comb in this shape. However, you can often find similar ornaments in the floral supply section where they sell wire, Styrofoam, or artificial flowers. One large feather or flower can be used to create a quick-and-easy decoration.

Appliqué

Pre-embroidered appliqués offer another pos-sibility for an extensive variety of custom-made combs. Look for them in packages or small drawers in the notions department. Simply glue one or a combination of several on the combs.

Organdy and pearls

This is another easy, but dramatic way to dress up a hairdo. Cut an oval piece of organdy (pink) and a matching piece of Stitch Witchery, an iron-on facing that makes the material slightly stiff. Fuse them together with a hot iron.

Cut slits in one long end of the material to the middle of the oval. String a beaded pearl on the ends of the cut strips. They will stay in place.

Glue the uncut end of the organdy piece to the top of the comb front and let dry. This creates a delicate fan-like ornament.

Crayon carrier

This item is designed for a child to take traveling or out to play. It is complete with pockets to hold a pad and a pack of cards and has spaces for organizing crayons. The outside is trimmed with a cloth measuring tape so the child can use it to measure straight lines. It is personalized with iron-on letters. Use heavy canvas or the back of a director's chair cover.

Materials: 1 piece of canvas 8 × 26 inches, 1 package of ½ inch elastic, 1 measuring tape, heavy duty thread, 1 piece of felt, package of iron-on letters.

Directions: Turn each long edge to the inside and stitch. Turn each short end in ¼ inch and fold 2 inches to the inside. Stitch across.

Cut a piece of felt 4 × 4 inches and another 3½ × 3½ inches. Place the canvas strip horizontally with the wrong side up on your work table. Make a pocket for a 3 × 5 inch pad by stitching three sides of the larger piece of felt to the canvas approximately 3 inches in from one short end. Make another pocket approximately 1 inch from the other. This will hold a pack of "Old Maid."

Cut two 5 inch lengths of the elastic. Beginning 3 inches from the end opposite the pockets, place one elastic vertically across the canvas. Pin across at 1 inch intervals and stitch a line at these points (see diagram). When the carrier is finished, space fat crayons 1 inch apart and insert them under the elastic.

Start at one corner and stitch the measuring tape down one side of the front of the canvas. Bring 7 inches up and around the end to create a handle and continue stitching the tape down the other side. Bring it up 7 inches over the other end and secure it at the corner where you started.

Attach iron-on letters (use initials or nickname when the name is long) according to package directions.

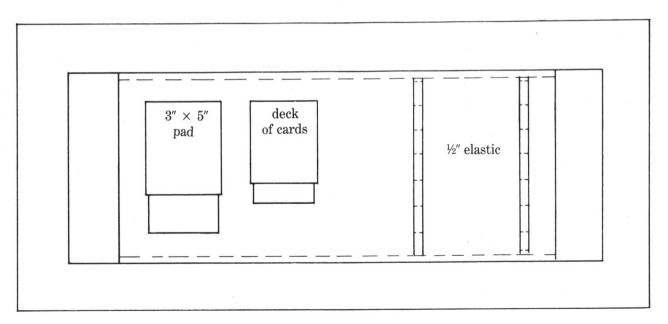

Barnyard table setting

These quick and easy cross-stitch projects are perfect for a lazy summer afternoon. If you want to while away the hours on the beach or visiting friends these are the perfect take-along crafts. See the project on page 155 for cross-stitch directions. This is the easiest and most foolproof needlework being done today and these designs have been adapted for contemporary use. The hen and her chicks on the place mat and napkin, and the duck on the potholder will bring a touch of country charm to your kitchen or dining area. **Materials:** Enough grid designed fabric for a mat 11 × 17 inches and a napkin 17 inches square, yellow and white embroidery floss, embroidery hoop, needle, scissors.

Directions: To make the place mat cut a 12 × 18 inch rectangle of fabric and hem it all around. Using 6 strands of floss in the needle, cross stitch the design about an inch above the lower edge. Press on the wrong side after all cross stitch is finished.

To make the napkin, cut an 18 inch square of fabric. Turn all edges under ¼ inch twice, press and stitch the hems by hand or machine. Cross stitch the design in one corner about an inch from the edges.

A country pot holder

Select a brightly colored graph fabric or gingham to make an ample sized pot holder. It's easy to create and you'll find this a perfect bazaar item as several can be made in practically no time. Very little material is needed so consider the leftovers from the project on page 155. The duck design used for the cross stitched napkin and summer coaster proves to be just as appealing on this project.

Materials: ⅓ yard of graph-check or gingham fabric, 6 strand embroidery floss (white used here with yellow for the feet and bill), polyester batting, needle, 5 inches of twill tape.

Directions: Cut two 10 inch squares from the fabric and two pieces of batting slightly smaller.

Mark a square in the middle of the front of one fabric square approximately 4½ × 5½ inches. Work a cross stitch frame around this square. Within this frame, work a cross stitched duck according to the counted cross stitch design provided.

Pin batting to the wrong side of each checked square. Stitch ½ inch from edges. Fold the twill tape in half lengthwise and pin to the pot holder front centered at one edge with right sides together and edges even. Stitch across the ends.

With right sides together stitch around three sides. Trim excess material and batting from seam allowance and turn right side out. Turn open edges in and slipstitch.

Symbol	Color
⊡	yellow
◺	green
◿	pink
⊠	blue
⬤	dark blue
☐	white

Needlepoint coasters

These small coasters are ideal take-along needlepoint projects. They'll fit anywhere, the designs will go fast and you can make several sets to give as gifts. No blocking is necessary as they are made from plastic needlepoint squares which come in a package of a dozen found in the notions department.

Materials: 4 inch square plastic canvas 7 stitches-to-the-inch, scraps of 3-ply yarn, tapestry needle.

Directions: Follow one of the charts and work the needlepoint in the Continental Stitch (see stitch guide page 48). To finish off this project, use a binding stitch around the outside to create a border. You may have to go around twice. Add a piece of felt or cork to the bottom if you like. This can be attached with white glue such as Elmer's Glue-All.

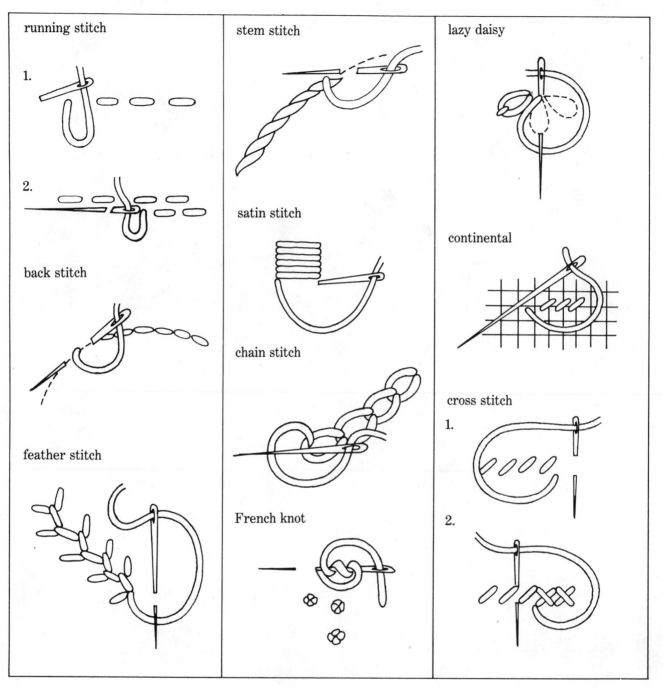

running stitch

1.

2.

back stitch

feather stitch

stem stitch

satin stitch

chain stitch

French knot

lazy daisy

continental

cross stitch

1.

2.

Basic stitches

48

Organizers

See-through organizers

Plastic sweater boxes and shoe boxes are always practical as they are fairly sturdy, stack well, and come in two or three sizes. Since they are transparent, it's easy to see at a glance what's in them.

Dress up a closet with stenciled words on each one. It's one way to guarantee that everything will end up in its place. Every time you open the closet you'll feel terrifically well organized.

Materials: plastic boxes, sheet of stencil letters (art or school supplies), tube of black acrylic paint, sponge brush, tape, tracing paper, pencil.

Directions: Tape the tracing paper to one side or one end of the box and pencil the stencil letters to spell out the word. In this way you can plan the spacing to fit.

Remove the tracing and tape it to the inside of the box to use as a guide. Place a piece of masking tape across the box as a guide for staying on a straight line.

Hold the stencil sheet in position on the box and stencil the first letter in the following way. Put a little paint in a shallow dish and tap the brush on the paint. Tap off excess paint onto a piece of paper and fill in the stencil letter. Wait for it to dry before moving on to the next letter. Acrylic paint dries quickly but if you place the stencil sheet over one damp letter in order to work on the next you run the risk of smudging the paint.

50

Stenciled box

This is another version of a file box. (See page 147.) This time the box is painted in a background color to match the wrapping paper lining. You can use Con-Tact or wallpaper as well. For this project I used one of the new peach tones. The stencil design is enlarged from the paper chosen for its simple repeat pattern. When selecting your paper, keep this in mind.

Materials: acrylic paint for background and designs, sponge brush, wrapping paper, white glue, a manilla folder (office or school supplies), X-Acto knife, pencil, plain paper, ruler, scissors, spray varnish.

Directions: Paint the outside of the box as well as the inside rim on the lid and the bottom. It may need two coats to cover. Enlarge a section

First color is tapped on with stencil brush.

of the design in the following way:

Draw a ¼ inch grid over the design to be enlarged. Make another grid with 1 inch squares on plain paper. Copy the original design onto the 1 inch grid square by square. If it's too big for the file box the design should be enlarged on a ½ or ¾ inch grid.

Transfer the design to the front of the manilla folder which will become the stencil. To transfer the design first go over the lines with a heavy pencil. Place this face down on the folder and rub over the back of the drawing with the pencil. Cut out all outlined areas with an X-Acto craft knife.

Mix the acrylic paint colors to match the designs in the paper. Hold the stencil cutout on the box and apply the paint to the open areas. If there is more than one color, apply paint to all the areas that are the same color, let dry and then apply the next color to those areas that require the second color and so on. When the paint is dry, the box can be lined.

Measure all inside sections of the box and cut the paper slightly larger than the measurements. Paper tends to shrink when glued.

Spread white glue (Elmer's) on the back of each piece and place it in position. The bottom pieces for the lid and inside of the box should be glued last. Don't forget the bottom of the box. If there is any excess paper above the edges, cut it away with a razor blade once the paper is dry.

When finished, all surfaces inside and out can be protected with a coat of clear spray varnish.

Stencil dark colors over light ones.

Everyday cover-ups

The five and ten is the first place to go when looking for practical items like pads, notebooks, pencils, and such. Sometimes we forget that with a paper or fabric covering these plain objects can become less ordinary.

Buy a good selection of notebooks, paper folders, a pencil caddy, school box, and clip board and cover everything with Con-Tact, wrapping paper or wallpaper. If you combine different patterns in contrasting colors you can create interest.

Some tips for ease of application: Cut each piece slightly larger than the area to be covered so that paper can overlap edges. When cutting use a metal straightedge and razor blade. Rubber cement is neat and you can remove the paper and reapply it if you make an error. However, if you are more comfortable with glue use Elmer's Glue-All.

Good-looking desk file

You will find an assortment of fold-up cardboard office organizers that includes file boxes, storage cases, traveling file holders, and desk organizers. They are made of printed corrugated for holding standard items and they are cheaper than anything comparable. If you take the time to cover them with decorative paper or fabric you can have a completely coordinated and handsome office area. These items can be made to look as good as those which are custom-made for the paper boutiques.

Materials: wrapping paper, wallpaper or Contact, rubber cement, scissors or razorblade, ruler, cardboard foldup file, manila folders.

Directions: These items come unassembled and it is easier to cover them after they are set up. Use each side as a pattern and place it on the paper. Draw around the outer edges of each side.

Cut one long piece to cover the front, bottom and back leaving enough extra paper to cover the inside.

If you're not using self-adhesive paper, coat the back of each paper piece with rubber cement and set aside to dry. Coat all areas of the file holder with rubber cement and leave to dry. Attach each piece and smooth out any air bubbles with the ruler. If you make an error use rubber cement remover before lifting and replacing the paper.

Brown wrapping paper has always been considered a sophisticated covering on these and other items. Initials can then be stenciled (art supply or school section) in white acrylic paint on one corner of each item. When coated with varnish, any paper covering will have a slick, smooth, attractive finish.

Decorative news

A masonite clipboard is handy to have anywhere. The problem is, most practical items aren't good looking enough to keep in view. The lucite version is expensive. With a little spray paint and tape or self-adhesive paper you can make an inexpensive one look good enough to hang in a convenient place.

Materials: clipboard, spray paint, Con-Tact or colored tape (school supplies), scissors, a pad to fit on the clipboard.

Directions: Give the board two or three coats of spray paint in the color of your choice. Let this dry thoroughly.

The design used here was cut from Con-Tact paper with a geometric pattern. You might choose one that has flowers, a basket-weave or any other design from which you can create a border. Place the writing pad on the board and arrange the cut out pieces on the clipboard around the pad. Remove the pieces one at a time. Peel away the wax backing paper and attach the decorative piece to the board. Continue until the area has been filled to your satisfaction.

Select one of the background colors for a silk cord, ribbon, or yarn to hold a pencil.

Seed packet file box

A metal or wooden recipe box is perfect for filing seed packets after planting the seeds. The information on the back of seed packets is sometimes needed days or weeks after starting the seeds. Often we can't remember when to transfer the starters to the garden or how deep to place them in the ground or whether to put them in the sun or shade. And last of all we can't remember where we put the empty packets if we remembered to save them at all. The answer is to file them. A seed packet fits perfectly into a recipe file and you can arrange them alphabetically with any information you want to add on file cards. The decorating technique used here is decoupage.

Materials: recipe box, greeting card or empty seed packet, small sharp scissors, white glue, damp sponge, spray or canned varnish. (Acrylic paint and a 1 inch brush are required if you want to change the existing color of the box.)

Directions: Paint the box if desired. Cut out a design from a greeting card or the front of a seed packet. Use a design that fits well on the box.

Spread white glue (such as Elmer's) on the back of the paper cutout and attach it to the box. Pat down firmly and wipe away any excess glue with the damp sponge. If the design goes from top to bottom over the opening, slit along the opening with a razor blade after design is dry.

Apply two or three coats of varnish to all surfaces. The inside can be left as is, or be painted or lined with wrapping paper.

Portable writing case

A regular straw or plastic straw place mat is the basis for this pencil carrier. You can plan it to hold as many items as you want. It can be a roll-up pencil box for a child or used for organizing artist's brushes to take along. I like it because it rolls up for easy travel or storage and can be hung over a desk for easy access.

I first saw this project being carried by a French school child. It held some of the most interesting calligraphy pens and colorful pencils I've ever seen. This project seemed easy enough to recreate.

Materials: 1 straw place mat, 1 package of blanket binding, 3 yards of 1 inch wide decorative ribbon.

Directions: Lay the place mat on a table and arrange the items on top of it. Plan to include pencils, pens, an eraser, a small ruler, scissors, even a compass if desired.

Cut two lengths of blanket binding and ribbon each 20 inches longer than the depth of the mat. Place the ribbon in the center of the binding. Leave 10 inches and weave the rest in and out of the straw on both ends approximately 5 inches from each outer edge. Every few inches catch the items tightly under the binding and ribbons.

When you reach the end, weave the binding and ribbons back through the straw and secure them. Roll up the mat from the top down and tie by bringing the blanket binding around to meet the ribbons on either end. For a Christmas gift tuck a sprig of holly under the ties. Use red and green ribbons.

Organized sewing basket

Baskets of many sizes and shapes are a good buy in the five and ten. Sometimes they fill an entire section, and in some stores they are part of garden supplies. This round tight-weave basket has a removable lid.

Materials: round straw basket with lift-off top, strawberry pin cushion (notions), package of ½ inch elastic, heavy thread, needle, scissors.

Directions: Cut a length of elastic to fit the inside circumference of the basket, allowing a ½ inch extra for each spool of thread to be inserted.

Baste the elastic to the basket, leaving ½ inch intervals loose where the spools will fit under the elastic. Leave another ½ inch space for inserting a small scissors.

The thread will be organized around the inside edge of the basket, leaving the basket free to hold other materials.

Secure the pin cushion to the top of the lid with a few tacking stitches.

Designer planters for under $5

Elegant clay pots

There are many kinds of plant containers that are commonly found in garden departments and most of us are familiar with them. The clay pots come in all sizes and lately I've found square and round ones as well as the traditional shape which is round on top and tapered at the bottom. They sell for just under $5 and the small ones cost under a dollar.

These pots are decorated with fabric flowers cut from a large floral cotton print. The secret to this project's success is in selecting a fabric design that fits the pots in size and color as well as good placement of the design elements. The pastel colors look especially good against the terra-cotta background.

Materials: cotton fabric, clay pots, sharp scissors, white glue (such as Elmer's), tape, damp sponge, clear spray varnish (such as Krylon).

Directions: Cut out all flowers, leaves, and other design elements from the fabric. Arrange a pleasing pattern on and around the pots, adding or snipping away parts of stems, leaves, and buds to make everything fit together.

Tape each fabric piece to the pot while arranging. Remove each piece one at a time. Spread glue over the back of the material and secure it to the pot.

Press down with a slightly damp sponge. This will remove any excess glue. Let dry. Apply several coats of spray varnish to the entire planter, allowing each to dry before applying the next. This protective coating will allow you to put the planters outdoors.

Metal flower box

These green metal containers are often used as window boxes. They come in 3 sizes all for under $5. You can use the green background or easily change the color with spray paint.

This project is a fine example of how the pastel flowers from the same fabric used on the clay pots (pages 62 and 64) look good on the dark green background. This time the arrangement is more dense, with the flowers placed closer together.

See previous page for materials and directions.

Ivy bucket

The previous projects utilized the standard types of plant holders. There are, however, many options that are equally inexpensive and good looking. You can use baskets, buckets, wastebaskets, garbage pails, and whatever else you find that is the right size for your plant.

The design of trailing ivy is created with decals applied to an ordinary pail with a handle. This gives you the opportunity to hang the plant if desired.

Materials: 1 package of border decals (comes in

one continuous strip by Myercord), scissors, damp sponge, clear spray varnish (if plant holder is used outdoors).

Directions: If you can't find decals, substitute a wrapping-paper design that can be cut and glued to the bucket. In order to make the ivy curve and form graceful lines, the decals must be cut apart here and there as you apply them.

Cut several strips of different lengths so you have some 6 to 8 inches long, others 2 to 3 inches long. Place them in a shallow bowl of warm water for 2 or 3 minutes. Remove them one at a time and slide the decal away from the strip of paper.

Adhere them to the bucket so the vines begin at the rim of the bucket and extend down the front. The idea is to create the look of an overgrown plant. Add pieces of the ivy here and there, making each piece curve in a pleasing way. You can overlap or cut away pieces and the cut lines won't show.

Pat each decal in place to remove excess water. Let dry before coating several times with varnish if the planter is to be used outdoors.

Berry-covered planter

You can find a plain, very large plastic plant holder for under $5 which seems like quite a bargain. These plastic pots come with a detachable tray on the bottom and are made in many colors, sizes, and shapes. With the addition of a decoration they are easily transformed to gift store status.

The design used here is cut out of cotton fabric. As with the projects on pages 62 and 64, fabric offers a wealth of possibilities in color and design. The berries are a bit more delicate to cut out and there is a large surface to cover.

When the cutout is delicate, with lots of thin stems for example, you will find it easier to manage if you cut it apart and glue a small piece at a time. In this way you can build up to the larger overall design.

When all pieces have been attached, spray the entire planter with varnish. Let this dry and recoat to protect the surface. The planter can then be used outdoors.

Herb carrier

Create a window box for little pots of herbs, or starter plants. When clustered together they are quite pretty and you'll have the added plus of fresh herbs to snip when needed.

The square and preferably low baskets are best for this project. This one measures 10 × 11 inches and is 3 inchs high. There is a handle on either side.

Nothing was done to the basket itself, al-though you could spray paint it if you want a color rather than the natural rattan. Look for a basket that has a loose rather than tight weave. Simply thread a row of ribbon in and out all the way around. Tie a bow in front where both ends meet. Use decorative ribbon or contrasting colors or all one color. The ribbons used here are ½ inch wide. Lace seam binding is attached to the top and bottom rim with white glue.

Name your plants

This time a green metal window box is given a coat of spray paint. (See other window box project on page 64.) The stenciled letters create a nice graphic effect. The spray paint is shiny and waterproof, and the acrylic paint used for the letters dries quickly and is equally waterproof for outdoor use.

In order to create a nice balance of color, use red or pink acrylic paint on a glossy white background if the window box is planted with geraniums. This makes a strong statement and is in keeping with the summer theme that goes with these flowers. Change the colors to suit the plants you use, if other than geraniums.

The window boxes come in 3 sizes and are made of green metal. This one sells for $4.99.

Materials: metal window box, white spray paint, sheet of stencil letters (art or school

Sketch word on tracing paper to make sure it fits.

Tape tracing in position as a guide.

supplies), red or pink acrylic paint, sponge brush, masking tape, clear fast-drying spray varnish.

Directions: Give the box two coats of paint. The surface will be smooth and shiny if you follow the directions provided on the can.

Put a piece of tape across the front of the box to use as a guideline. Hold the stencil sheet on the box and fill in each letter. (See page 51 for more detailed directions.) Don't put too much paint on the brush and dab rather than stroke it on. When the paint from the first letter is dry move the stencil sheet into position for the next letter. Work from the outside edges toward the center of the cutout stencil area to avoid paint seepage under the stencil. If some red paint gets on the white where it shouldn't be, it can be touched up with white acrylic paint and a pointed artist's brush.

When the paint is dry, give the box a coat or two of spray varnish. This last step is optional as the spray enamel and acrylic paint are permanent. However, if the box will be used outdoors the varnish adds protection.

Beads, bangles, buttons, and bows

Ribbon pillow

It has become fashionable for the better boutiques, lingerie departments, and bed-and-bath shops to carry scented sachets, pillows, and a good assortment of pouches filled with potpourri.

Depending on the size and intricacy of the craftsmanship, the prices can be very high. Some of the pillows and bags are made from antique lace, silk, and moiré with wide lavish ribbon trimmings.

This is such a foolproof project that it makes sense to consider it as a good gift to make. It will cost approximately $2 and certainly look much more expensive. The ribbons that are used here are not extraordinary but the more elaborate the ribbons the more unusual the item.

Materials: 1 yard ½-inch white satin ribbon, 1 yard ½-inch decorated ribbon, 1 yard 1-inch purple satin ribbon, 1 package 1-inch lace trim, 2 pieces of pink or white cotton fabric 5½ × 6½ inches, a piece of cardboard larger than the finished pillow size, tape, polyester filling or potpourri, drop of perfume.

Directions: Tape the edges of one piece of fabric to the cardboard. Start at one end and place 6 lengths of 6 inch strips of purple ribbon side by side vertically. Hold each strip in place on the fabric with a little piece of tape at the top and bottom of each piece of ribbon.

Cut five 6 inch pieces of white ribbon and four 6 inch pieces of decorative ribbon. Begin at the top and weave one strip of white ribbon in and out of the purple. Tape at each end. Weave a row of decorative ribbon and keep alternating colors until the square is completely covered.

Carefully remove the tape as you pin the other piece of fabric to the ribbon-covered fabric. Stitch around all edges, leaving 2 or 3 inches open. Turn right-side out. Fill lightly with perfume-scented polyester or potpourri. Do not overstuff. Slip stitch opening.

Edge the entire pillow with a double layer of lace trim, stitching as close to the ribbon edges as possible.

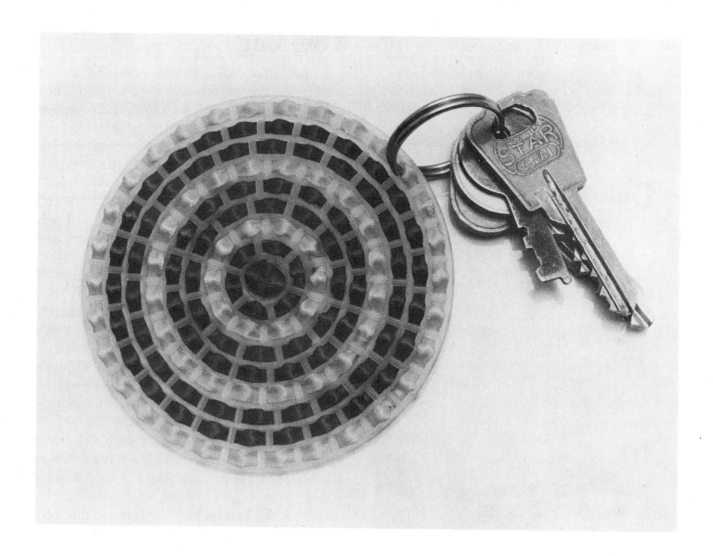

Key holder

It will be hard to lose your keys with this key holder, which is approximately 3 inches in diameter. Round plastic canvas comes in a package of a dozen. They are commonly used for needlepoint coasters and come in a variety of square sizes as well. As a departure from needlepoint designs, ribbon weaving is less time consuming and offers a new look.

The ⅛ inch ribbon is made by the Offray ribbon company and comes in a wide assortment of colors so you can make up any combination. Select 2 or 3 colors and weave rows of alternating ribbons. Leave an inch at the beginning and end to finish with a knot at the back. Clip as close as possible.

This project is especially good as a bazaar item because you can easily make several and the variety of colors will suit anyone's taste. Make them as gifts or party favors.

Tote bag

A package of ordinary open-weave dish towels is a terrific five and ten cent store bargain. They come in a package of 3 for about $1.30 and you can make any number of interesting items from one, two, or three. No one will ever guess what the item is made from or for how little money.

Each time I bought a package the dish towels were slightly different, but basically similar. They come in white or beige with a stripe of red, green, blue, and yellow across the top and bottom. The material looks like cotton crochet and is perfect for weaving ribbons or yarn to fill the open weave. If you're not sure what they look like, you'll recognize them immediately when you see them. It's the kind of item that's easily overlooked until you need to buy them.

Materials: 2 dish towels, 4 packages Offray's ⅛ inch satin ribbon in colors to match stripes on towels, 1 package of small wooden beads (notions).

Directions: Turn in one end of each dish towel and place them together with the turned ends to the inside. Line up side edges. Use one color ribbon to weave in and out of the dish towel, attaching the bottom and the sides of the tote. No sewing is required.

Weave alternating ribbon colors in and out of the fabric, leaving an open row between each color. You can fill the entire bag with ribbon or simply do a few rows.

To create a drawstring for the bag, weave one length of ribbon through the fabric beginning and ending on one side. Then weave another through from the other side.

Tie the 4 ends together to form a shoulder strap. Leave a few inches of ribbon hanging. Attach the wooden beads to the ends of each ribbon.

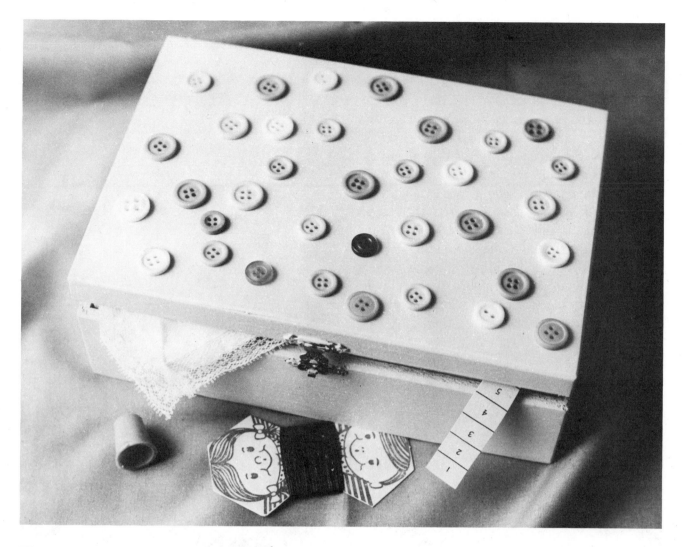

Button-covered sewing box

In many toy departments I've found a charming wooden sewing box for a young child. The box is painted either bright yellow or red and on the top it has a terrible printed picture of a little girl sewing. The best features of this item are the size (it is 8½ × 5½ inches), the hinged top, the clasp closure, and a lift-out divided compartment tray. The inside holds a little card of yarn, a paper ruler and a lace-trimmed cotton handkerchief with a stamped design to embroider. All this for under $5.

The first improvement is pastel pink paint.

Two coats are needed to cover the design. Buy 4 cards of sherbet-colored round buttons in peach, lemon, aqua, and blue. They have a matte rather than shiny finish and are quite pretty.

Glue them at random across the box. If you want to do more work line the inside with pastel wrapping paper.

While the box was originally intended for children it was not redesigned with this in mind. In fact, it is very handy for organizing writing papers, stamps, envelopes, and pens.

Decorative buttons

Wooden buttons come in several sizes and look good on bulky sweaters, jackets, and vests. Since the surface is smooth and plain you can create designs on them with cutout flowers and butterflies from greeting cards and wrapping paper. Each button can be different or all matching. This is a simple project but the buttons will give an ordinary store-bought article of clothing a handmade look. When decorated with small cutouts from a children's book, these buttons look especially nice on a child's sweater.

If you need a quick but interesting gift, make a set of the buttons for someone who knits or sews. Sew 4 or 6 on a card and wrap in a jewelry box (wrapping paper and card section). See page 107 for cardboard gift box idea.

Dressed-up bag

One of the fanciest shops in New York sells this bag for $85. As you can see there is nothing to it, except a very good idea. The nylon string shopping bags are marvelously versatile but not something we'd use for anything more than carrying parcels. Here it has been elevated in status with the addition of satin ribbon tied all over the front and back. Combined with its best feature, which is sturdiness, you will have a good-looking beach tote or a shopping bag to match any outfit.

The ribbons are ½ inch wide satin and you can use all one color, 2 or 3 colors that go together, or cover the bag with multicolored bows. I saw them in all combinations and one looked better than the next.

The bags come in pink, red, yellow, and sometimes white. They are folded in a little package not always easily visible. I found them most often at the check-out counter, but in some five and ten's they were hanging with the pocketbooks. If you don't see them ask for them. Every store carries these bags, as they are one of their most popular items for under $1.

Beaded necklace

The beads used on a ponytail elastic have especially good qualities. They are a nice size and come in clear or colored plastic that looks like glass or thick Lucite. The holes are not placed through the center, but as near the edge as possible. When strung on a silk cord, the beads hold in a good position that creates an interesting necklace. A package of 6 sets will give you 12 beads for little more than $1.

Half the beads in this necklace are covered with strips of paper to give them the irregular, soft-looking shape of handmade beads. The subtle colors of frosted nail polish are used to create a necklace of copper, apricot, pearl pink, or bronze. The lavender silk cord is used as a delicate contrast.

This style of costume jewelry is currently popular in the better boutiques, sometimes selling for over $100.

Materials: 1 package ponytail elastic, 2 or 3 colors of inexpensive frosted nail polish, white bond paper, white glue, 1 yard of silk cord.

Directions: Rip strips of paper 2 to 3 inches long. Dilute white glue in a bowl and add the paper strips. Place the glue-soaked strips around every other bead. Overlap the strips of paper and mold them to the beads to make them slightly larger and irregularly shaped.

Let the beads dry thoroughly. Coat the paper-covered beads with frosted nail polish, let dry and coat again. Repeat a third time if necessary. Cut the elastic and remove the beads.

Feed the silk cord through each bead, alternating between paper-covered beads and plastic beads, and tie with a knot at spaced intervals. The overall length of the necklace, once tied at the back of the neck, is 12 inches.

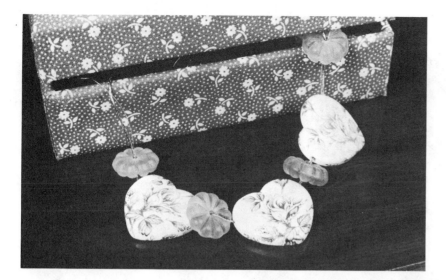

Costume jewelry

Heart necklace

These beads are unusually pretty. The large floral hearts are ceramic and the raspberry glass beads are shaped like flowers.

Each store carries a different variety of beads that can be strung on nylon fishing or picture-hanging string (notions or hardware). The clasp is usually sold in notions.

Flower bead necklace

This necklace is made of 4 large white wooden beads decorated with small decals and tiny paper flowers from the department where combs and headbands and barrettes are sold. They are also available at Easter time where baskets and trimmings are placed.

The decorations for the beads can be self-sticking seals, little hearts that are sold before Valentine's Day or cutout paper flowers from wrapping paper or greeting cards. The bunch of flowers is separated and 2 or 3 stems are inserted at each end of the beads after they have been strung. String this necklace with ⅜ inch royal blue satin ribbon. The project makes a sweet accessory for a flower girl to wear. Or add this to an Easter outfit.

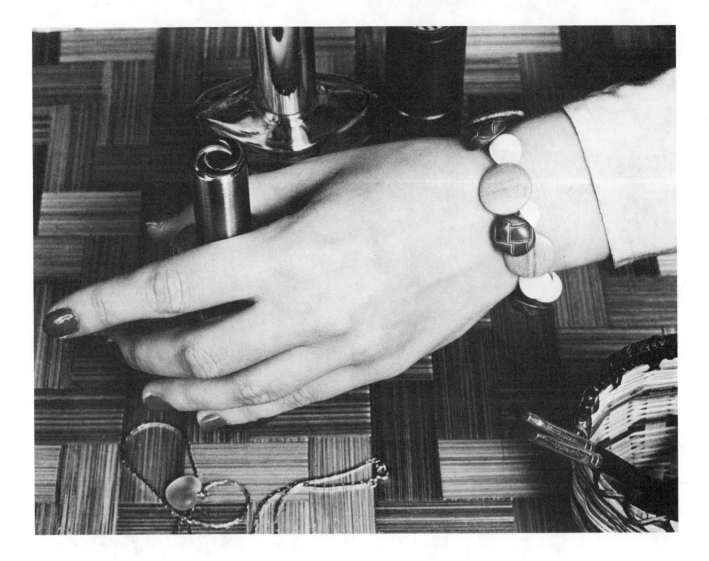

Button bracelet

Everyone seems to have an odd assortment of buttons. This is a good way to put them to use. String as many as you can on nylon thread (notions) cut to fit your wrist. This project looks best when different sizes, shapes and colors are bunched together.

If you haven't purchased buttons in a long time, you'll be surprised at the variety available. Design your own jewelry quickly and inexpen-sively. Because buttons are so varied you can create jewelry that looks more expensive than junky, depending on your selection.

In this case I combined round brown wooden buttons with round-shaped white buttons. These are not flat buttons with holes through them, but the kind that one attaches from underneath. They are found on better garments. The small clasp is also available in the notions department.

Fashion finds

Fanciful summer hats

The following started as plain, inexpensive straw beach hats with a rope cord or uninteresting band glued around the head. This kind of project is irresistible because the simplest trim applied with minimal efforts brings big returns. It has to be one-of-a-kind, it is personally altered to your colors and taste, and it is really fun to wear. I don't know why it is, but the easiest and often most spontaneous creations of this sort seem to bring the most satisfaction.

The easiest thing to do with a straw hat is to wrap and tie it with an interesting ribbon. I used a purple paper ribbon with silver hearts printed all around it and tied a full bow on one side.

The next one is first wrapped with floral ribbon. Artificial flowers are then glued to the ribbon and brim. White glue does the trick.

The third hat is my favorite. The design is a cutout fabric flower that is glued to the hat. A shocking pink ribbon band finishes the look. To protect the fabric give it a quick coat of clear spray varnish. This will also keep the straw in good shape.

Camisole

It takes three dish towels, or one package, to make this summer camisole that will cost under $2. Narrow satin ribbons fill the open-weave area and you can do as many rows as you feel are necessary. The finished strapless top looks like it has been crocheted. (See project on page 74.)

Materials: 3 dish towels, 4 packages of Offray's ⅛ inch ribbon, 1 package of ½ inch elastic, needle and thread.

Directions: Sew the ends of 3 dish towels together to create a tube. Alternate ribbon colors and weave in and out of every other row of the fabric.

Weave the elastic in and out of the top row of the material and tie the two ends together at one side. Cut off excess elastic ends and pull the fabric over the knotted section. The elastic will blend right into the weave.

If you want to add straps, cut 3 or 4 pieces of ribbon in different colors for each side. Gather the ends together and stitch in place at the front and back so they fit over the shoulder.

84

Jellybeans

Inexpensive rubber shoes that look like sandals come in pale colors and clear, for children and adults. Originally worn at the beach, "jellybeans" have become popular summer shoes to be worn anywhere. Make a pair of party shoes for under $5.

Materials: Jellybeans shoes, 2 yards each of ¼ inch satin ribbon in two different colors (peach and pale green used here), scissors.

Directions: Weave the ribbon in and out of the open work around the toe of the shoes.

Tie the ends of the ribbon in a bow where they meet at the point of the toe. Weave the other color ribbon in and out and tie a bow above the first. Alternate ribbons until you have a row of bows up the front of each shoe.

Save some ribbon to tie around the lace of ankle socks.

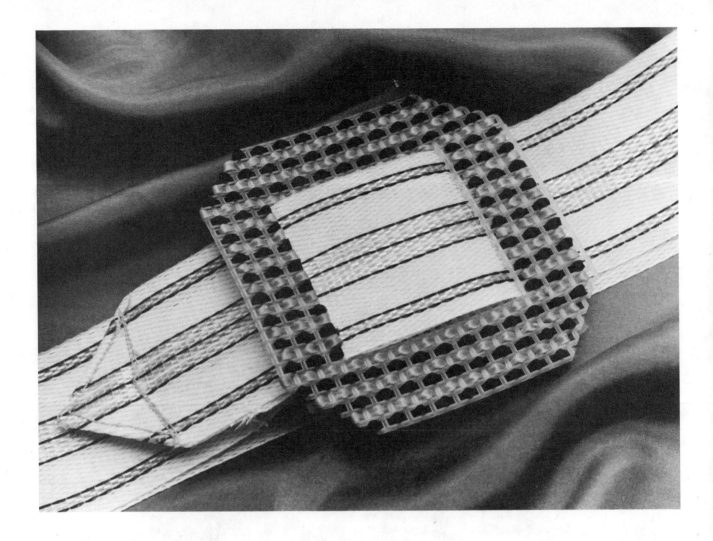

Distinctive sport belt

Plastic webbing for lounge-chair repairs comes in a package containing 13 yards for under $1. You'll find many bright colors as well as black and white. When you look at this material out of its context, it has some interesting qualities. The design is contemporary and the woven plastic looks like metallic thread. There are many possibilities for this item, used as a decorative trim (see page 50), and here, combined with other elements as a belt.

Materials: 1 package of Re-Web kit, 1 plastic 4×4 inch needlepoint canvas (notions or arts and crafts), 2 packages of 2 different colored ⅛ inch satin ribbon (Offray Co.), heavy-duty thread, razor blade.

Directions: Measure your waist and add 10 inches. Cut that length of webbing.

Cut the triangles off of each corner of the plastic needlepoint canvas 5 rows from the point. To make slits on the canvas to hold the belt, count down 6 rows from the top and 6 rows in from each side. Use the razor blade to cut down this row, ending 6 rows from the bottom edge. Make corresponding cut on the opposite side.

Fold one end of the webbing ½ inch to the wrong side. To attach the webbing to the buckle,

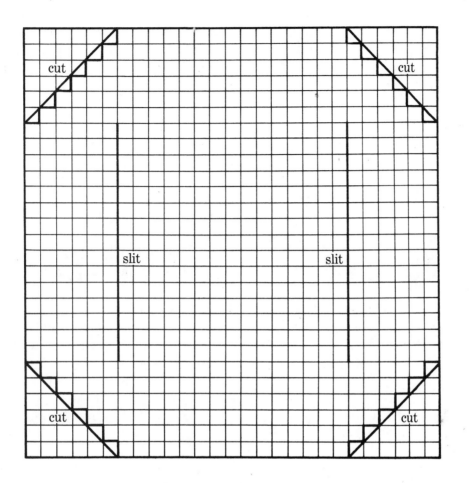

feed this end through both slits in the canvas. Fold 3½ inches of the webbing back and stitch it to the front of the webbing.

Fold down 3 inches of the other end of the webbing and stitch it to the belt. Fold both corners of the end of the webbing to the back, creating a pointed belt end. Stitch closed.

The basic belt is complete and can be worn as is. The canvas can be filled in with a border of yarn or with ribbon as shown here.

Weave ¼ inch ribbon in and out of the stitch holes, alternating colors. Tie loose ends at the back of the canvas and clip as closely as possible.

Bandanna skirt

You can whip up a skirt for a child or yourself in fifteen minutes and for under $2. It's perfect to wear over a bathing suit and can be folded to the size of a hanky.

Materials: 2 large cotton bandannas (they come in purple, yellow, navy, and red), 2 yards of 1 inch wide grosgrain ribbon same color as bandanna or contrasting color.

Directions: Turn a top hem of 1 inch to the wrong side of each bandanna and stitch, leaving each end open. This is the channel through which the ribbon will be fed.

Pin right sides of bandannas together. Begin 2 inches from the bottom edge and stitch each side together ending at top hem line. Since all edges are prefinished no more sewing is needed.

Cut the ribbon in half. Attach a safety pin to one of the ribbon lengths and feed it through one channel. Repeat with other ribbon through the remaining channel of the skirt. Tie the ribbons on either side of the skirt to close.

For a larger size sew 1 or 2 more bandannas together and create a drawstring closing around the top.

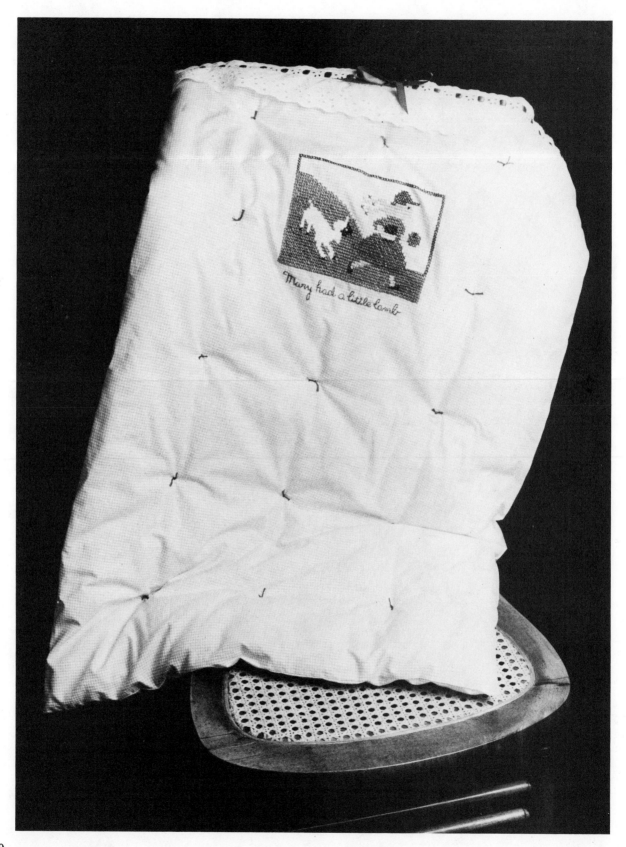

Carriage quilt

A gingham quilt with a nursery illustration is the perfect gift for a new baby. The cross-stitch design can be worked very quickly and it takes just one yard of fabric with enough left over for a pillow sham. Gingham comes in many pastel colors with different size checks. Here we used the smallest grid pattern. The finished quilt measures 32 × 22 inches.

Materials: 1 yard yellow gingham, 24 inches of wide lace trim, Mountain Mist polyester quilt batting, DMC embroidery floss in the following colors: red, pink, white, orange, brown, blue, green and black, embroidery hoop, fine needle.

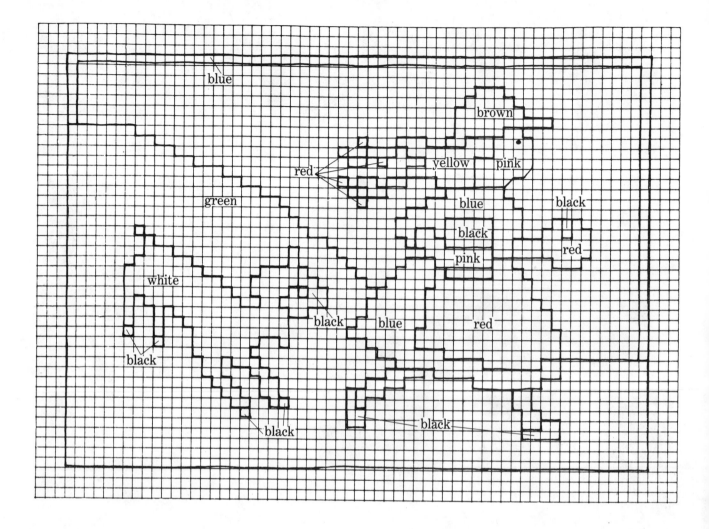

Directions: Cut the fabric in half lengthwise and cut 3 inches from the end so you have 2 pieces 33 × 22½ inches. Follow the diagram to position the cross stitch design.

Always use an embroidery hoop while you are working and remove it from the fabric when not in use. With 2 strands of floss in the needle, work the cross-stitch following the chart. (See page 155 for cross-stitch details.) Never knot your embroidery floss when beginning and ending. Since the gingham fabric is quite thin do not pull the thread too tightly as you work to avoid bunching. When the design is complete pad an ironing board and press from the wrong side.

Place the band of lace along the top edge of the cross-stitch fabric. Next place the piece of batting on top of the fabric over which will go the other piece of gingham face down. Pin and stitch up sides and across the top with a ½ inch seam allowance. Trim batting from seam edges and turn right side out. Turn remaining edges in, press and slip stitch.

Use 6 strands of embroidery floss to make ties at spaced intervals on the quilt. Follow the diagram for placement. Insert needle from front to back and up again, then tie in a knot leaving ½ inch loose strands.

Evening jacket

Ordinary pull-on sweat shirts come in pastel colors as well as gray, navy, and black. They are soft, warm, lightweight, and practical as well as inexpensive. For very little effort you can transform this garment into a Chanel-cut evening jacket.

Materials: long-sleeve sweat shirt, scissors, 4 yards of 1 inch wide white satin ribbon, 4 packages ⅛ inch satin ribbon (Offray Co.) in contrasting colors, needle, thread, pins.

Directions: Cut off ribbed sleeve ends and waistband. Cut down the center of the shirt front. Turn all raw edges under and stitch a finished edge.

Stitch the 1 inch wide ribbon down each side of the opening, around the neck and the bottom edge.

Pin strips of ⅛ inch ribbon across the front of the jacket on corresponding sides of the opening beginning approximately 2 inches down from the top of the neckline. Each strip is about ½ inch apart and there are 7 rows. The ribbon rows should end at the arm seamline.

Edge each sleeve at the wrist with the 1 inch ribbon. Beginning ½ inch from the top edge of the ribbon, pin rows of ¼ inch ribbon around each sleeve. There are 4 rows of different colored ribbons on each sleeve. Hand stitch the ribbons to the sweat shirt.

Striped clutch purse

This clutch purse is simple enough to make in the morning and use in the afternoon. The only sewing required is on the side seams. The stripes are created with iron-on seam binding (Wm. E. Wright Co.) and if you use Stitch Witchery you can eliminate all sewing. The pattern is a simple rectangle and the diagram is provided to create the design.

Look at the variety of colors found in seam binding and create your own combination. The red, white and blue used here makes a bold statement.

Materials: piece of muslin 12×16 inches, 3 packages of iron-on seam binding (if you can't find iron-on binding use a sheet of Stitch Witchery which is a fusible web also found in notions).

Directions: Turn all edges ¼ inch and press. Follow the diagram for placement of binding and alternate the colors so you have a white stripe between every red and blue stripe. When the fabric is completely covered run a band of blue around the outside edges.

Fold one short end up 5½ inches to the inside and press. Stitch along each side edge to attach front and back of the purse. Edge the remaining inside flap with blue seam binding to finish and fold down over the bottom portion. Press. Add a decorative clasp or leave as is.

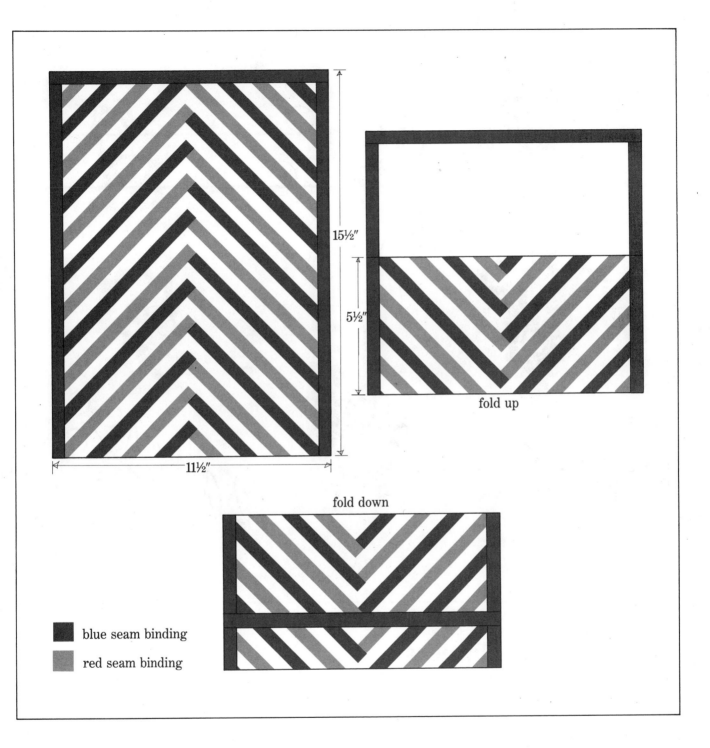

15½"

11½"

5½"

fold up

fold down

blue seam binding

red seam binding

Embroidered slippers

Chinese slippers have become popular because of their comfort and versatility. An embroidered appliqué, fabric paint, or beaded trimmings make each pair unique.

If you tack the appliqué in place, you can change the design often to go with various outfits. These pre-embroidered appliqués come in many sizes and the design categories include flowers, fruit, shapes, animals, and hobbies.

Look for them in notions.

Iron-on appliqués are another possibility but the designs are more limited. You can also create an original design to be embroidered.

Four appliqués are used here, costing under $2. The shoes range in price from $2.99 to $7. In this case one butterfly appliqué is used on the sock with a corresponding butterfly on the shoe.

Painted berry basket

Lace sachets

Fabric flowers on Parson's table

Paper cutouts on Parson's table

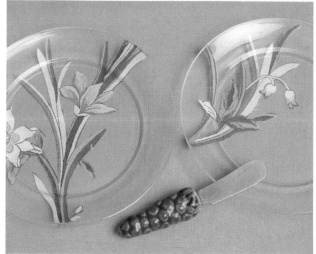

Fabric flowers under glass

Decals and doilies on breadboard frame

Hankies, ribbons and lace make $4 tablecloth

Fabric-covered metal flowerbox

Place mat with abstract crayon design

Stencil letters transform flowerbox

Fabric scraps and ribbon pin cushion

Boutique necklace for $2

Button bracelet

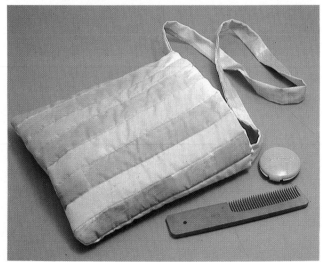

Quilted tote bag

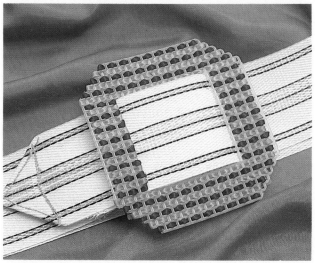

Needlepoint canvas buckle/webbing belt

Ribbon weave key holder

Simple needlepoint coasters

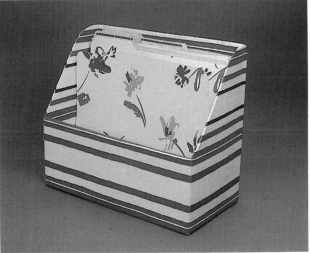

Paper-covered file holder

Transform cardboard storage pieces

Greeting card cutout on file box

Ribbon sachet

Mushroom purse from felt squares

One-step bandanna skirt

Lace hankie, ribbon and appliqué sachet pillow

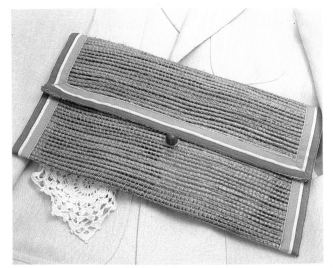

Straw place mat turned into a clutch purse

Quick-and-easy country pillows

Scrap craft holiday decoration

A transformed Sucret tin

Ribbon bows turn Jellybeans into party shoes

Fabric cutouts decorate planter

Ribbon belts

Any ribbon can be used to make a belt; if you find a well-stocked ribbon department, the possibilities are endless and cheap. Match any color. Dress up a solid color outfit with an exquisite ribbon pattern. I found similar ribbon belts in a New York department store and they were selling for $12. As you can imagine they will cost considerably less to make.

Materials: Enough ribbon to go around the waist plus 8 inches, belt buckle (notions).

Directions: To secure both buckle ends to the end of the ribbon, pull 1 inch of ribbon through the buckle and turn the raw edge under. Stitch across both layers of the ribbon.

Turn down the other ribbon end and stitch across. Fold in each corner to create a point and stitch on each edge.

To make a reversible belt, stitch 2 different ribbons together and attach to the buckles. Finish as above.

If thin ribbon is used, sandwich belt stiffener (notions) between 2 lengths of ribbon.

Don't throw it away

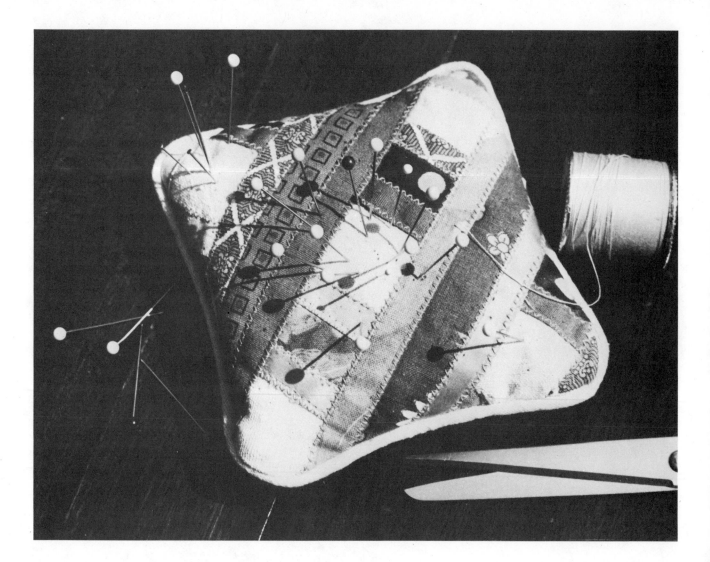

Scrap pin cushion

You probably have all the materials needed for this project in your sewing basket. If not, you can find interesting remnants or use ribbons to make this little pin cushion. It is 4 × 4 inches, so very little material is needed.

Materials: enough ribbons or scrap material to cover a 4 inch square area, 2 pieces of plain cotton fabric 4½ inches square, 16 inches of cording, polyester fill.

Directions: Pin strips of material to 1 plain square of fabric following the pattern in the photograph if necessary. Any way you arrange them will look good. Stitch all edges of the strips to 1 piece of the backing material.

Turn edges on all 4 sides of the fabric-covered piece and the backing piece, and press. With wrong sides together pin the 2 pieces with the piping cord between. Stitch all the way around leaving a 2 inch opening. Stuff the little pillow until it is quite full. Stitch opening.

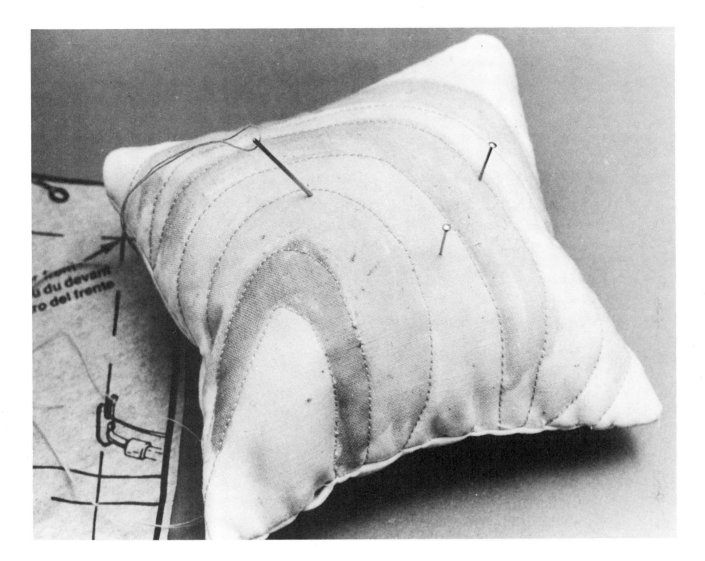

Rainbow pin cushion

Make a batch of little pin cushions to sell at a bazaar. They're easy to make and will sell quickly for $2 apiece.

The technique is crayon transfer (see projects on pages 24 and 39) and the design is freehand coloring. Any abstract pattern will look good or you can use a design that isn't too detailed.

Materials: small piece of white cotton fabric, polyester batting and loose filler, Crayola Craft Fabric Crayons, needle and thread, iron, white

Bond paper, newspaper, scissors.

Directions: Cut 3 pieces of fabric 4 × 4 inches. Cut 1 piece of batting slightly smaller.

Draw a 4 × 4 inch square on the Bond paper and crayon a loose rainbow of colors within the area.

Put a few layers of newspaper on your ironing board and place 1 piece of fabric on top. Lay the crayoned paper face down on the fabric. Set your iron to cotton and press down on the paper to

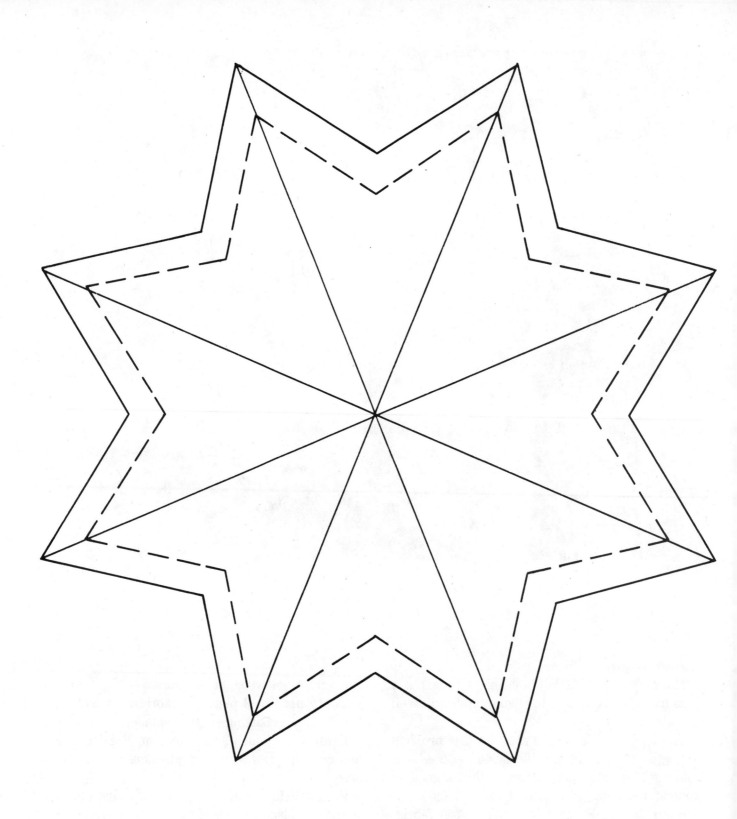

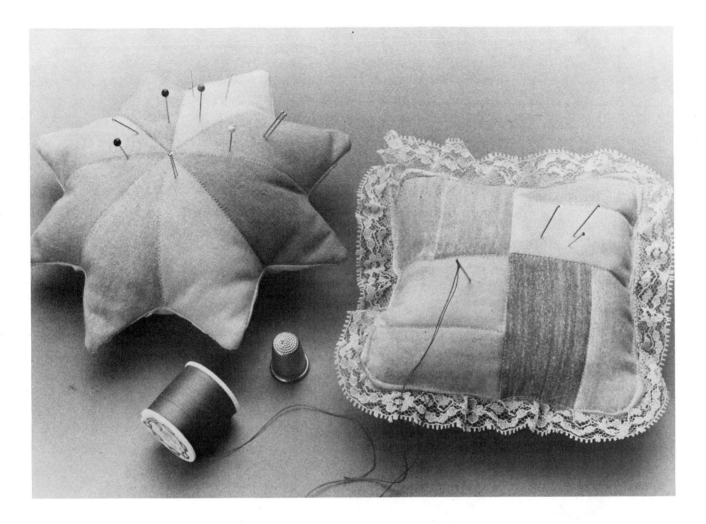

transfer the rainbow. The colors will appear pale pastel.

Sandwich the piece of batting between the crayon fabric and another square. Stitch each line to quilt the rainbow. Pin the third square of fabric to the front of the design and stitch around 3 sides. Turn right side out and press. Stuff the little pillow with filler and turn the raw edges in. Stitch the opening.

Star-shaped pin cushion

The star-shaped pin cushion is created in the same way. Simply trace the design and cut out 3 star shapes from white cotton. Color each section of the paper star pattern with a different crayon and place it face down on one piece of fabric. Transfer with a hot iron. Remove and finish as

with previous project. This can also be used as a Christmas tree ornament.

Patchwork pin cushion

The patchwork pin cushion is made in the following way. Measure off 8 rectangles $1 \times 2\frac{1}{2}$ inches on Bond paper. Color each section a different color. Cut them apart and arrange them face down on a $4\frac{1}{2} \times 4\frac{1}{2}$ inch piece of fabric. Transfer the color with a hot iron as above. Quilt and stitch the front to the back piece with a border of lace between if desired.

To create more simple designs, trace shapes from a coloring book and transfer them to fabric in the same way. This technique is fun, easy, and the results are always rewarding.

Cactus pin cushion

A pin cushion doesn't have to be small and easily misplaced. This one stands on its own, providing easy access for quick repairs. It also looks cute on a sewing table. Just one 9×12 inch piece of green felt is used to make this 6 inch high pin holder.

Enlarge the pattern provided here and cut out 2 pieces. Pin the felt together and stitch around the outside as close to the edge as possible leaving 2 to 3 inches open.

Fill the cactus with polyester batting and finish stitching it closed.

Put the cactus pin cushion in the center of a flower pot and fill around it with decorative stones (fish tanks and supplies). Stick pins all over the cactus.

Pineapple centerpiece

Turn a pineapple on its side and you have the body and tail of a rooster for your next Thanksgiving centerpiece.

The head is made from one 9 × 12 inch piece of red felt. The pattern pieces are cut with pinking shears. Use a bit of leftover braid, ribbon, lace and rick rack to trim and a decorative bead or button for the eye.

Enlarge the pattern provided here and cut out two pieces. Cut two narrow strips 2 inches long to fit under the beak. Pin the 2 pieces of felt together with the strips in place and stitch around all edges, leaving the widest edge open. Stitch a band of gathered lace around the opening and add a band of black braid. Sew a bead or button where indicated on the pattern for the eye. Slip the finished project over one end of a pineapple and arrange on a plate.

Paper bag planter

This idea couldn't be cheaper or more fun because it's a takeoff on an idea found in a more elaborate form in gift shops and even art galleries.

Crumple a regular brown paper bag, then open it up. Fold down the top edge about an inch. Squash the bag down slightly so it can stand freely but is a little lopsided.

Spray the bag inside and out with clear, fast-drying acrylic, such as Krylon. Let dry. Add several more coats, allowing each to dry. When spraying move your hand back and forth in one section so the paper is saturated but not dripping. After 5 or 6 coats the bag will begin to stiffen. After 10 or 12 spray coats the bag will have a hard shiny surface and the creases and wrinkles in the bag will be permanent. The whole thing will look like a piece of ceramic. It will also be waterproof enough to hold a plant.

If you use a small lunch bag, it can serve to hold pencils or dried flowers on a desk. To expand this idea further, try it with a large supermarket bag. It makes a terrific wastebasket. Or spray paint it first, then coat with acrylic.

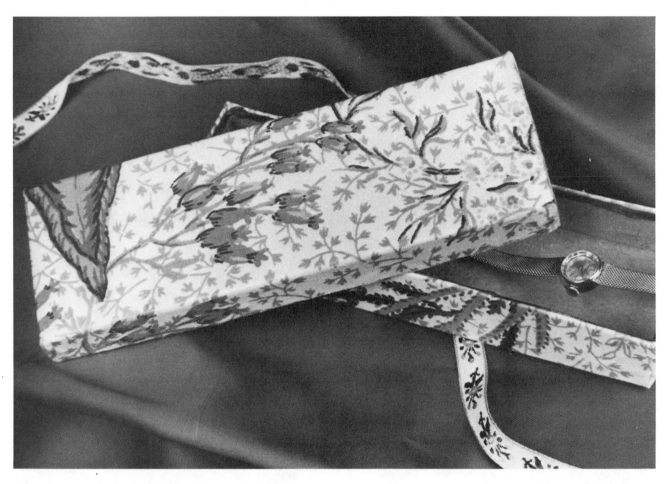

Fabric-covered jewelry box

This is not an original or unusual project, but one worth mentioning since it's a good idea. If you have a piece of jewelry to give as a gift, turn the gift box into a jewelry box that can be used on a dresser.

There are many colorful fabric prints to choose from in the five and ten. While this may not be the first place you'd go to find fabric, a remnant can often cost as little as 25¢. Often the prints aren't as nice as you'd find in a fabric shop, but when you're using so little sometimes the most overdone or busy print can look well designed. A simpler print might not look as good on such a small item.

Materials: cardboard jewelry box, enough fabric to cover outside surfaces, white glue, 1 piece of felt in a color to match one of the colors in the print, scissors, ribbon (optional for inside trim).

Directions: Use the box as the pattern, and place each side on the fabric. Draw around it and cut out each piece. The fabric pieces will be slightly larger than the areas to be covered.

Glue each piece to the box, overlapping at edges and over the rim to the inside. Cut pieces of the felt for the inside bottom and sides, but not the top. Glue the sides in first, then the bottom piece. Glue the ribbon around the top edge to finish. Protect the fabric with Scotchgard, or leave as is.

Not for notions only

The flower is not painted on this lid although in reality this looks like a hand-painted box. A transparent plastic notions box is easily decorated from the inside out.

Materials: pale yellow acrylic paint, red poppy wrapping paper (or any paper with a large bright design), white glue, scissors.

Directions: Cut out 1 or 2 paper flowers to fit the box lid. Cover the front of the designs with a thin film of glue. Press to the inside lid so that the design shows through when the box is closed.

Smooth down the paper with pressure to force the excess glue out at the edges. Let this dry for a few minutes.

Use a piece of a sponge or a sponge paint brush to dab (not stroke) the paint onto the inside lid coating over the back of the paper as well. The paint will not cover all areas on the first application, but the acrylic is fast drying.

When dry, dab more paint over the area until it is completely opaque.

Trinket box

If any of you have read my other books, you've probably discovered that they each contain a trinket box project. My first book was on the craft of decoupage and the little ring or trinket box became my trademark. You can use any small container such as a covered soap dish, pin box, or powder box for this project.

The process is decoupage and is applied in the same easy way that was used to make the Seed Packet File Box on page 57.

Materials: container, light blue acrylic paint, brush, 1 large paper flower (cut from the front of a seed packet, greeting card, or wrapping pa-per), scissors, glue, damp sponge, spray or can of varnish.

Directions: Paint the box inside and out and let dry. Coat again. Cut out 1 large flower to fit on the top of your box. Coat the back of the design with glue and attach to the box. Pat away excess glue with a damp sponge.

If the design overlaps the opening, wait for it to dry, then cut across the opening with a razor blade. Give the entire surface a coat of varnish. If you use spray varnish, you can apply 4 to 5 coats in an hour. The canned varnish takes 24 hours to dry but is equal to 3 spray coats.

Travel sewing box

An empty Band-Aid box makes a delightful sewing or mending kit carrier for the college bound. It's also a good last-minute gift. Fill it with sewing aids for a Christmas stocking stuffer.

Materials: Empty Band-Aid tin, paper doily, pink acrylic paint, brush, white glue, clear nail polish or spray varnish, sponge, small piece of felt, polyester fill for padding inside lid, small piece of cardboard, scissors.

Directions: Paint the entire outside of the empty Band-Aid box. Prop the lid open while drying. When the paint is dry, apply another coat for complete coverage.

Determine the placement of the doily and coat the back with white glue. Handle the paper carefully so it won't rip as you place it on the front of the box. Pat down all areas with a damp sponge.

Let dry before covering the sides, back, and top areas. Cut away any overlapping and excess doily. Let the paper dry thoroughly.

Coat the entire surface with clear nail polish or spray varnish. One or 2 applications will give the box a shiny protective finish.

Lining: The inside is lined with pink felt. Small squares are available in many colors in the notions department. Trim the top edge with ribbon. The box can also be lined with wrapping paper or Con-Tact. If you use paper, seal with a coat of clear nail polish or varnish after it has been glued in place.

Pin cushion lid: Cut a piece of shirt cardboard to fit loosely inside the lid. Remove the cardboard and pad one side with polyester fill (cushion dept.) or 2 or 3 cotton balls.

Cut a small piece of felt or delicate cotton print slightly larger than the cardboard. Cover the filler with the felt or fabric and overlap the edges to the underside of the cardboard.

Coat the inside lid with glue and set the pin cushion in place. It should not touch the hinges at the back so the top will close. Press down and set the box aside to dry with the lid open.

110

Lacy sachets

Little pouches to hold sweet-smelling potpourri can be made from any delicate material. However, for a romantic look combine pale pink lace, purple velvet or satin ribbon, and embroidered appliqués.

In this case each sachet is made from the top portion of a whole slip. The lace cups are lined with taffeta and you can make 4 or 5 little bags from the top alone.

Materials: 1 slip (or 2 pieces of fabric 4 × 5 inches for each sachet), ½ yard of ½ inch ribbon, embroidered appliqué (notions), mixture of potpourri made from dried petals, package of lace seam binding.

Directions: Cut the material so you have 2 pieces for each bag. Since the shape of the bra part of the slip is not square, work with it to create a strawberry or heart shape. It seems to fold easily into these shapes.

With right sides together stitch up sides and across bottom of the material. Turn the bag right side out. Stitch the lace to the top edge while gathering the material to create a ruffle.

Hand sew the ribbon around the bag approximately 1 inch from the top edge. Leave a few extra inches where you begin and end the stitching of the ribbon to tie the sachet closed.

Add embroidered appliqués to the front of each sachet. You can decorate them with sequins, rhinestones, ribbons or beads, all available in notions.

111

Holiday doorknob cover

At Christmastime when everything in the house is undergoing a transformation it can be fun to decorate the doorknobs as well. This is an easy project to whip up just before a party and it will certainly attract attention. It is not meant to be practical and you might want to use it on a knob that doesn't receive constant use.

Materials: 1 piece of red felt, 1 piece of green felt, little piece of elastic, red thread, thin pliable wire (hardware or floral section), cluster of plastic berries, scissors, safety pin. Optional: green satin ribbon, bells.

Directions: Cut a circle of red felt 2 inches larger than your doorknob. Turn ½ inch under and stitch, leaving a little opening to insert the elastic. Attach a safety pin to one end of the elastic and feed it through the channel. Tie the ends together and stitch the opening closed.

Use the pattern provided and cut 6 leaf shapes from the green felt. Cut small pieces of wire to fit down the center of each leaf. Put 2 pieces of felt together for each leaf and stitch around the outside edge with red thread. Leave a tiny opening at the base of each leaf.

Insert the wire and stitch down the center of the leaf on either side of the wire.

Overlap the bases of the 3 leaves and stitch them to the center of the doorknob cover. Sew the little plastic berries to the center of the leaves where they come together. Slip the cover over your knob and if you like, tie satin ribbons around the doorknob as well. Add silver bells to the ends of the streamers.

Variations

Use the larger leaf pattern to create the variation and the previous directions for cutting and stitching the red circle and green leaves. Overlap the bases of each leaf and tack in place at one edge of the red cover.

The Joy doorknob cover makes a statement with cross-stitch on red Aida cloth.

Materials: Small piece of #10 Aida cloth, white embroidery thread, needle, embroidery hoop, piece of colorful cotton print 3 × 16 inches, small piece of ¼-inch elastic.

Directions: Follow the cross-stitch chart and use 3 strands of floss to create the letters in the center of the fabric. Cut a circle around the word so it is 2 inches larger than the doorknob. Finish as per directions for felt cover.

Cut a long strip of fabric on the finished edge to avoid making a hem. Gather the fabric by basting the raw edge approximately ½ inch in. Stitch this to the underside of the edge of the doorknob cover.

Slip the finished project over the doorknob and add a red ribbon tie.

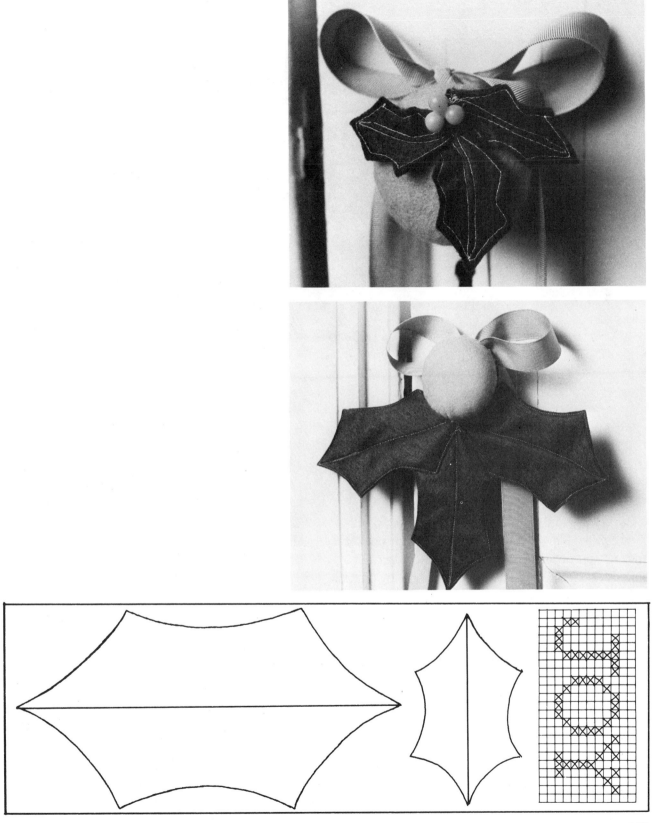

Pill boxes

Sucret or candy tins are good sizes to hold pills or vitamins. They fit easily into a purse or pocket and can be decorated in a variety of ways. The elegant boxes shown here were made by J.R. Trzcinski and are an example of how an ordinary item can be designed in a sophisticated way.

The technique is decoupage and the paper cutouts come from wrapping paper, greeting cards, or similar sources. The directions here have been simplified from the traditional decoupage method for quick and easy crafting.

Materials: Sucret tin, acrylic paint, small brush, clear varnish or nail polish, paper designs, cuticle scissors, white glue, sponge.

Directions: Paint the outside of the box, including the hinges and bottom. Let the paint dry, then apply a second coat. The background color used here is royal blue.

Select and cut out paper illustrations that will fit on the lid. Glue each one in place. Pat away excess glue with a damp sponge. For a variation you can use stamps, stars, labels, seals, or heart stickers as designs. Check the school-supply sections for more ideas. Consider covering the lid with rows of white buttons if it is to hold buttons or pins.

Coat the entire box with varnish or nail polish and let dry with the lid propped open slightly. Apply 2 or 3 more coats allowing each to dry between applications.

The inside can be left as is, or painted or lined with paper.

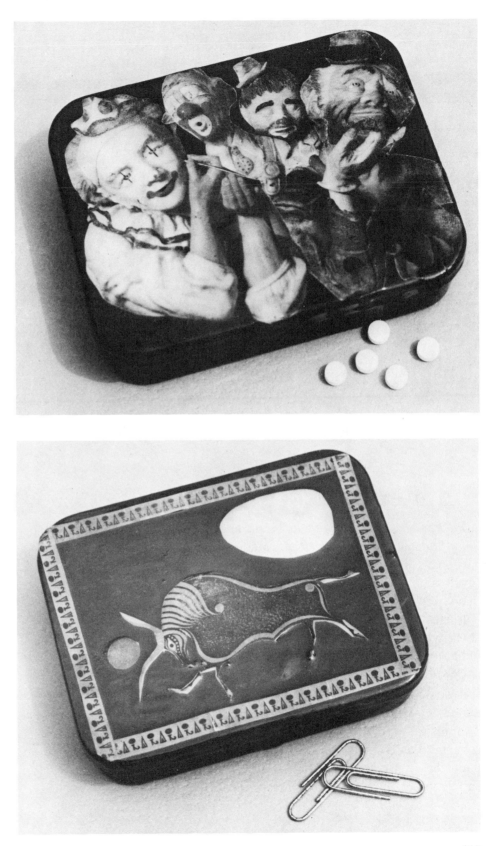

Put it in a bucket

Paper paint buckets come in 3 sizes and can be found in most hardware sections. Made of sturdy cardboard they make excellent containers for toys, yarn, desk and kitchen utensils. Since their main purpose is to hold paint they are fairly waterproof and make good plant pots. Decorate them with cutout illustrations, decals, or spray paint.

These have been designed for a child's room. One holds the loose items such as crayons, blocks and cars, the other holds a bunch of fall flowers. The designs were cut from vinyl Wall-Tex wallcovering but you can use Con-Tact or wrapping paper or greeting cards. Stick-on letters (school supplies) can also be used to personalize each child's catch-all. This is a good way to organize mittens or socks.

Instant
inspirations

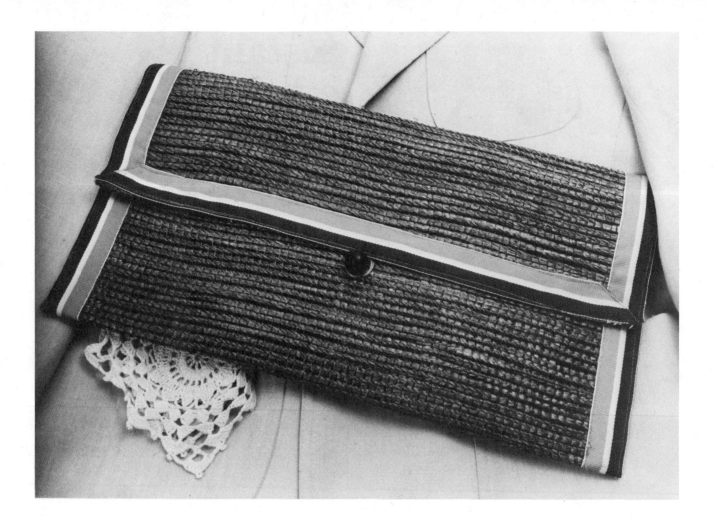

Clutch purse

Straw place mats cost approximately $1.50. They are natural in color or you will find them in bright summer colors as well. The one shown here is bright green and the ribbon trim is a stripe of green, white, and pink. You'll need one rectangular mat to make this clutch purse. This is a simple half-hour project. There are many ways to add variety each time you wear it. If the trimming is tacked on, it can be exchanged for another whenever you change outfits.

With the wrong side up turn ⅔ of the length of the place mat over on itself and pin at the sides. Pin 1 inch wide decorative ribbon around the edges and stitch the front and back and ribbons together.

Continue to trim the rest of the outside edges. Add a little ribbon twist to the top flap and a corresponding bead or button to the bottom portion. The decorative rose is made of paper ribbon and found with wrapping paper and greeting cards. Add a piece of Velcro to close the purse. Or add embroidered appliqués to the purse for another look. The open weave lends itself to embroidery or ribbon weaving as well. Have some fun mixing and matching ribbons, place mats, and trimmings.

ribbon rose clasp

plastic needlepoint canvas with ribbon weave

pre-sewn applique (notions).

Straw planter

This has to be one of the best five and ten cent store projects of all. Number one, it costs $2.49. Number two, it is useful beyond what it was intended for, as a hat. Number three, it's good looking as a plant holder. Number four, it costs less than any basket originally intended for this purpose. And number five, I didn't have to transform it in any way.

Just turn any rolled brim straw hat upside down, insert a small saucer and plunk the right-sized plant into it.

120

Christmas photo ornaments

Wooden curtain rings make interesting tree ornaments. The rounded natural wood creates a small frame which can be left as is, stained, or painted. It is shown stained here. There is a little screw eye in each for easy hanging. The wooden ring can frame a little needlepoint picture or a photograph.

Materials: Package of wooden curtain rings, photos slightly larger than the hole, small piece of felt (notions), glue, ribbon for hanging, scissors, pencil.

Directions: Place the ring over each photograph. Adjust it to frame the area you want to use. Draw a circle around the outside of the ring on the photograph.

Cut out the photos so they are slightly smaller than the drawn circle. Put a thin line of glue around the back of the ring and set it on the photo. Press down and leave to dry.

Cut out a piece of felt smaller than the ring. Coat the back of the photo and frame with glue and place the felt down.

Use yarn or thin ribbon for hanging on the tree. You can make one for every member of the family, adding an ornament each time there's a new arrival.

Personalize a party

Take advantage of throwaway plastic cups and glasses to personalize your next party. Each person might have a cup with his or her initial on it, or use stick-on letters to spell out your message. An after-the-game party? Cups proclaim "We Won!" or "Hoorah!" or "Cheers! for No. 1." Add some gold sticker stars around the gold and black letters. Look for these stickers in school supplies.

To Stencil Cups: Cardboard stencil sheets can be found in school or art supplies. Tape the stencil to the area on the cup and fill in the letter with acrylic paint.

Add a simple stem of flowers. This can be done freehand as the idea here is to make it festive and any decoration will make these throwaways look better.

Another idea is to decorate each cup with a band or two of colored Mystik tape. Choose the colors of the winning team.

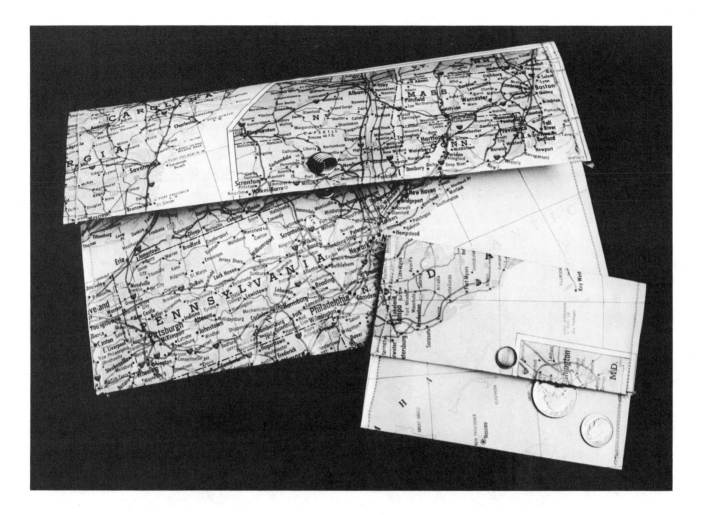

Map case

It's handy to have a folder to hold maps in the glove compartment of the car or even in a drawer at home. Use a map and clear plastic Con-Tact paper to create a handsome and useful gift. It's surprisingly sturdy as well.

Materials: A new map that is folded flat rather than with many folds, 1 yard clear Con-Tact paper, heavy duty thread, 1 snap (notions), scissors, ruler, pencil.

Directions: Open the map and cut a portion of it to measure 11 × 20 inches. Cut two pieces of Con-Tact the same size.

Sandwich the map piece between both pieces of Con-Tact. With wrong side up fold each short end up 3 inches. Smooth to create a crease.

Turn the bottom portion up 5½ inches. Stitch along both side edges from bottom to top edge, stitching front and back together. Fold top edge down 3½ inches over the front of the case.

Secure corresponding sides of the decorative snap closure to the top front of the flap and the bottom portion of the case.

Use a scrap piece that was cut away from the map to make a small toll change purse to leave in the car. This one measures 4 × 5½ inches. Make it as per directions for map case.

A fifteen-minute apron

This apron is made from two bandannas with half of one left over for a pocket, potholder or neckerchief. It takes about 15 minutes to make.

Materials: 2 bandannas, 2 yards of 1 inch wide grosgrain ribbon to match.

Directions: Cut one bandanna in half from corner to corner creating two triangles.

With right sides together pin the raw edge of the triangle to one end of the finished bandanna. Gather and create easy folds in the material as you pin. The fabric should match up at the edges.

Stitch along the top edge. Open to the right side. Fold the top point of the apron to the inside and stitch across the top edge.

Cut an 18 inch length of ribbon and stitch each end to either side of the top of the bib to create an over-the-head strap.

Pin the rest of the ribbon to the front of the apron where the top and bottom meet, leaving equal lengths on each side for tying. Stitch across the top and bottom edge of the ribbon where it's pinned to the apron.

124

Dish-towel apron

One dish towel can be made into a decorative apron for practically no time, effort, or money.

Materials: linen dish towel, 3 yards of cotton cording.

Directions: Cut the shape of the top of the apron according to the diagram on the following page to create a 7 inch wide bib.

Wrap the fabric over the cord where the dish towel curves, leaving an extra ¼ inch for turning raw edge under. Remove cording and stitch the channel on either side.

Thread one end of cording through the channel at one side and down through the channel on the other side. Make a knot at each end of the cording. Pull enough cording up at the top of the apron to go over your head. Put the apron on and adjust it by sliding the material up or down on the side cording. Tie around your waist.

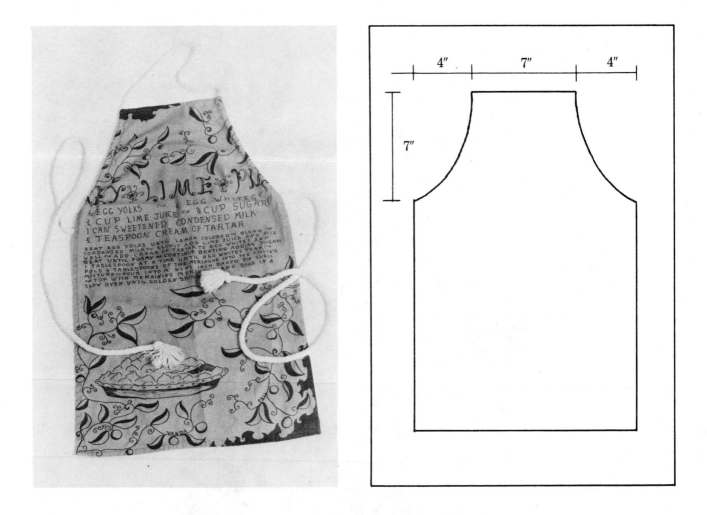

Bartender's apron

Make this shorter version of the dish-towel apron as per directions for previous apron. Cut off 5½ inches from the bottom of the dish towel. Hem the top edge of this strip. Turn the raw edge of the apron up on the right side and press.

Place the strip on the front of the apron so the bottom edges meet. Pin to the apron and stitch down both sides and across the bottom. Stitch down the center of the strip to create two pockets.

126

New ways
with artificial
flowers

Pencil boxes

Artificial flowers are what make these boxes and the following containers special. You can use any containers and floral combinations. The largest selection of flowers is found early in the spring.

These pencil boxes are plastic toothbrush and toothpaste traveling cases. Most often they are found in clear, pale blue, or light pink, but recently they have been made in more interesting colors like deep wine, ivory, dark green, and black. Look for them in the cosmetic section.

Materials: plastic box, 1 stalk or cluster of artificial flowers, white glue, scissors, 1 package of ⅛ inch green satin ribbon.

Directions: Take apart a stalk of artificial flowers and cut off the leaves. Arrange the flowers in a small cluster, or use one or two with some leaves.

After an arrangement has been determined, apply a generous amount of glue to the back of the flower and place on the top of the container.

The flower will hold if left to dry for an hour or more. The petals won't lie flat but will remain in the shape they were in on the stalk. Apply a line of glue down the spine of the leaf and place it so that one end is hidden under a petal. Do not disturb it while the glue is drying.

For variety make flower stems from ⅛ inch ribbon cut in varying lengths. Glue stems in place and add flowers to the top of each ribbon.

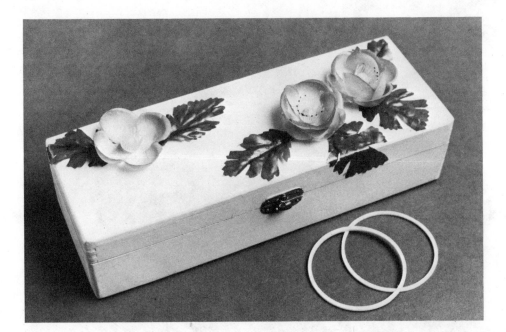

Flowering boxes

These boxes are made of wood, although the technique can be used on plastic tissue holders, soap dishes, metal file boxes, and cardboard gift boxes. I found these boxes in the arts-and-crafts section; however, most five and tens don't carry wooden boxes, so if you can't find them use others. The most frequently found wooden box is a recipe file for 3 × 5 inch cards.

Materials: box or container, acrylic paint if wooden box is used, brush, artificial flowers, white glue, scissors, wrapping paper for lining (optional).

Directions: Paint the box and let dry. A second coat may be needed. Take apart a variety of artificial flowers and cut off the leaves. Cut the plastic stem under each flower.

Arrange the elements on the top of the box before gluing them permanently in position. Apply a generous amount of glue to the back of the flowers and place gently on the box. Leave it to dry. Do the same with each leaf. If you want to add flowers to the front or sides of the box (as with the dogwood), wait at least an hour for the top flowers to dry. Turn the box on its side and apply the other flower.

Cosmetic jar

Sometimes the simplest design looks best and takes the least amount of time. I found some flowers in dusty colors of rose, aqua, and grey/blue. Two of the blue ones are on the wine-colored pencil box on page 128 and one rose-colored flower and leaf sit alone atop this little cold cream jar.

The plain little plastic containers sell for under $1 and come in several sizes and shapes. They make excellent cosmetic holders and look pretty when decorated and arranged together on a table or dresser top. (See page 132 for directions.)

This technique is especially good for recycling used cosmetic jars and little boxes because the colors are often interesting and the size of the packaging is useful.

A gift box

It would be misleading to call this project a soap dish, even though that's what it is. It can be used to hold candy, soap in the bathroom or kitchen, pins or buttons, paper clips or push pins, stamps, vitamins, or cosmetics. At any rate, it cost $1 unadorned and I thought it was such a good buy that I bought one each in green, red and yellow. The sprig of artificial dogwood for 39¢ can go a long way. By itself, holding nothing, it's a nice little gift box.

Pull one flower and leaves off the plastic stalk and apply a generous amount of glue to the underside of the flower. Set it on one corner of the box. Apply a strip of glue to the underside of the leaves and set them on the box with the base partially concealed under a petal. When all is dry, spray the flower with clear varnish. Let dry and spray again. This will stiffen and protect the design.

132

Flower frame

Frames are expensive. Even the plain black metal frames cost a lot, but are the least expensive and they are dependably available for any size picture. The problem is that they aren't very good looking. A scrap of cotton fabric, some acrylic paint and tiny artificial flower buds can change that.

Materials: frame, small tube of red and white acrylic paint, brush, a stalk of small blue artificial flowers and another of pink, spray varnish, scissors, rubber cement (school or art supplies), razor blade.

Directions: Remove the glass and cardboard backing from the frame.

Mix a small drop of red into a tablespoon full of white acrylic paint to get a pale pink. Give the frame 2 coats of paint, allowing the first to dry before applying the second.

Cut a piece of fabric the size of the cardboard backing. Coat the back of the fabric and front of the cardboard with rubber cement and let dry.

Carefully place the fabric over the cardboard and smooth down. Measure the photograph to be used. Using the razor blade, cut a square that's slightly smaller in the center of the fabric-covered board.

Touch up the inside edge of the cut square with the pink paint. Tape the photo to the back of the opening.

Cut the buds from the plastic stalks. Arrange them approximately an inch apart and glue them around the frame alternating the colors. Let them dry. Spray the flowered frame with 1 or 2 coats of clear varnish. Reassemble the frame and hang.

133

Blooming planter

A plastic wastebasket is perfect for a planter. It is sturdy, waterproof, and comes in all sizes, shapes, and prices. The one used here was chosen for its oval shape and yellow color, which is a good background for the white artificial flowers.

Materials: plastic wastebasket, artificial flowers, 1 package of ⅛ inch green satin ribbon (Offray ribbon company), white glue, clear spray varnish, damp sponge, scissors.

Directions: Cut or pull apart the stalk of artificial flowers to separate the flower from the plastic stem. Cut the leaves off.

Determine where the design will be placed. Cut lengths of ribbon for flower stems. Attach them to the container with white glue. Pat in place with a damp sponge, which will remove excess glue.

Apply a generous amount of glue to the back of the flowers and place one at the top of each stem. If there are layers of petals, glue the first layer, then each layer on top of that.

Apply glue to the back of each leaf spine. It needn't lie flat. The finished project will appear three dimensional. Let the flowers dry for about an hour.

Spray with a fine coating of clear varnish. This will stiffen the flowers and allow you to use the planter outdoors. Let dry between coats and apply 5 to 6 times. It takes minutes to dry.

Interior designs

Tablecloth

If you haven't checked out the handkerchiefs available in the five and ten lately, you're in for a treat. They range in price from three for a dollar to approximately $2.25 apiece and are as lovely as any hand-embroidered, lace-trimmed items that sell for five times the price. Use them as creatively as possible. (See page 26 for another project.)

Four large, colorful, and boldly printed floral hankies are used here to make this bridge table covering used on top of a larger plain white cloth. Add as many as necessary to fit your table. Combine colors and designs, but they should all be the same size for one project.

Each hanky is separated by a row of eyelet woven with ½ inch wide satin ribbon to match the hanky colors.

Arrange the handkerchiefs on the table top and pin a strip of ribbon or lace along the hanky edges. Stitch the elements together on the machine.

Use handkerchiefs for napkins as well. This is a quick, easy, and delightfully old-fashioned way to set a coffee table when serving afternoon tea or coffee.

For a children's party, make it seem formal with a lacy embroidered hanky tablecloth. They come already lace trimmed with a pastel embroidered bouquet of flowers in one corner.

When soiled, throw it in the washer and hang out to dry. It may look delicate but this project doesn't need delicate care.

Pastel patchwork pillow

Pastel colors are no longer the province of infants and young children. Ice cream-colored fabric, home furnishings, clothes, and accessories of all sorts are changing from the high tech colors of red, black, and white to a softer look.

Influenced by the new romantic feeling, hand-crafted projects are taking a turn as well. The new techniques being used help to create this look. We see it in painted baskets done with the palest peach, aqua, baby blue, and yellow and these more subtle colors in knit sweaters and crocheted afghans.

Fabric crayons also create these colors and the technique of transferring a loose crayon design is in keeping with this style. The patchwork project that follows is not made with extensive sewing and piecing of material but rather from one solid fabric that is made to look like patchwork.

Materials: 1 foam pillow form 12×12 inches, 3 pieces of white cotton or polyester fabric 13×13 inches, 1 piece of polyester batting same size, 1 package Crayola Craft Fabric Crayons (toys or craft section), several sheets of white Bond paper, pencil, ruler, scissors, iron, newspaper.

Directions: Rule off the Bond paper with 2-inch-spaced lines. Rule down the other way every 4 inches. Color in all the squares, alternating crayon colors. For a 12×12 inch pillow you will need 18 colored sections.

Cut the paper so that you have 18 individually colored pieces. Pad your ironing board with

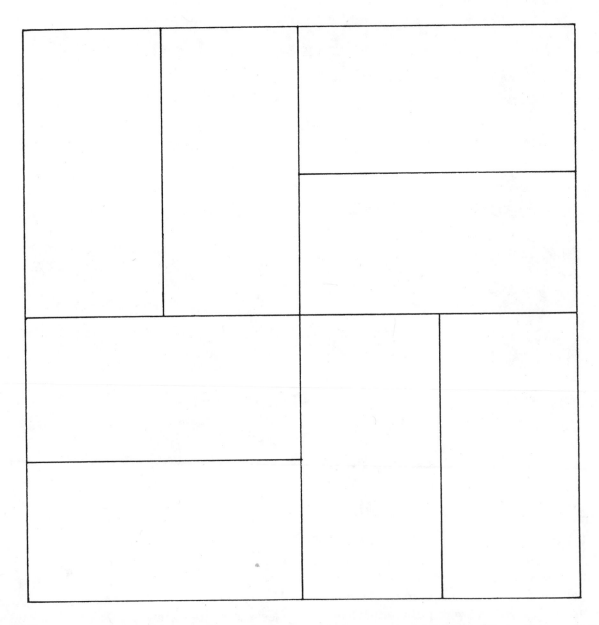

newspaper and place one piece of white fabric on top. Arrange the paper pieces crayon side down on the fabric. (See diagram.)

Set your iron to cotton and press it down on each crayon section. Do one piece at a time. Remove each piece as you transfer the color. You can only use it once unless you reapply the crayon to the paper. Once the design is transferred to the material it is colorfast and will not run, fade, or disappear in the wash.

With crayon side down place the polyester batting on top of fabric. Then place a piece of plain fabric on top and pin together. Sew between all color rectangles to create the quilted patchwork.

Pin the last piece of cotton to the front of the crayoned piece and stitch around all edges, leaving enough open for turning. Clip seams as close as possible. Turn right side out and press from the back. Any excess color will come off onto the newspaper. Stuff with the polyurethane pillow and slip-stitch opening.

Country style pillows

These quilted pillows may look like appliqué but are actually much easier to make and the results couldn't be more deceiving. Even up close anyone would believe that the designs were either applied piece by piece or hand painted. These pastel country motifs are made with fabric crayon transfer that is as easy as coloring a picture in a child's coloring book. Everything you need is available in the five and ten.

Materials: white cotton or polyester fabric, polyester batting, Crayola Craft Fabric Crayons, newspaper, Bond paper, lace trim, cording (optional), tape, 14 inch polyfoam pillow form or stuffing, needle and thread.

Directions: Begin by enlarging or tracing the design from the book. As you can see the designs are repeated 4 times to create the overall pattern

large enough for the pillows.

To transfer designs: Place several layers of newspaper on your work surface. Do not work directly on a hard table. Color in the designs. In this case the color combination is red and green which, when transferred becomes much softer in color than it appears on the crayoned paper.

Brush off all specks of crayon that have formed on the surface of your coloring and surrounding areas. You can't use the same coloring more than once therefore you'll need a colored design for each section to be transferred.

Cut 3 pieces of cotton fabric 16 inches square and a piece of batting slightly smaller. Draw a 14 inch square within one fabric square to contain the design.

140

Pad your ironing board with several layers of newspaper and iron it flat so there are no creases or folds in the paper. Set the iron for dry cotton. Place the squared off piece of fabric face up on the newspaper and tape it down at each corner. Position each of the 4 colored designs (all the same) on the fabric. In other words, if you are using the basket design you will have crayoned 4 papers with this same design. You may have to cut away excess paper on each to position it with the others. Once in position on the fabric tape each corner of each design to the fabric.

Hold the hot iron over one section at a time for about 3 to 5 seconds, lift and move to another section. Do not move iron across the paper but rather press and lift. To check the transfer carefully lift one corner of one design and peel back. If more color is desired in a specific area reheat without moving the paper so that the design will stay in register.

Pillow construction: Once the designs have been transferred to the fabric they are colorfast. Sandwich the batting between the designed fabric and 1 piece of cotton and pin at each corner. Quilt on the machine or by hand by stitching around the outline of the designs. I used white thread to clearly define each element.

Finish: To finish the pillows you can add lace trim, a ruffle of fabric to match one of the colors or cording to pipe the edges. Pin these elements to the front of the pillow following the penciled line on the fabric. Pin the remaining square of cotton on top of this and stitch around 3 sides. Trim seams of excess fabric and batting and turn right side out. Turn remaining edge to inside and press.

Fill the pillow with stuffing or a polyfoam pillow form and slip stitch opening catching the lace or ruffle trim between the front and back of fabric.

Each square equals 1″

142

Pot holder: This project is made from one design square. Cut 3 squares of cotton fabric ½ inch larger than the design. Sandwich a double layer of polyester batting between the front and 1 square and stitch around edges. Quilt by stitching around the design.

Place the last piece of fabric on top of the design and stitch around 3 sides leaving one corner open. Fold a piece of 5 inch grosgrain ribbon in half lengthwise and insert at the open corner. Turn raw edges in and slip stitch closed. Reinforce the corner with the ribbon.

Decorator dessert plates

Inexpensive glass plates are used to create elegant dessert dishes. While they look like they have been handpainted, the design is created with fabric. With this method each plate can be one-of-a-kind. Make one to use as an ashtray or candy dish.

Materials: Cotton print of large flowers, scissors, white glue, clear spray varnish, glass plate, sponge, butter knife.

Directions: Cut out the fabric designs. Spread a thin film of white glue over the front of the cutout. Press it in place on the bottom of the plate. With a butter knife, start at the center of the design and smooth to outer edges. Excess glue can be removed with a damp sponge. As the glue dries, the white film will disappear.

Spray the bottom of the dish with a light coating of clear varnish. Repeat two to three times. Use these dishes on a solid color tablecloth to match or contrast with the colors in the design.

Do not submerge the plates in water. Wash carefully by hand. However, they are not as delicate as they look and will take normal use.

Christmas decoration

There is a large variety of baskets found in most five and ten cent stores and they are reasonably priced. For this project look for a large weave with flat surfaces rather than a tight rattan. If the basket will be hung to hold greens on the door or Christmas cards by the hearth look for one that has a flat back and handle. Some baskets are made for this purpose.

The natural color and texture give this decoration a country look but if you prefer it can be painted with spray or acrylic paint before adding the stencil design.

Materials: natural basket, stencil paper or manila folder, stencil brush, craft knife, pencil, red and green acrylic paint. All materials are available in the art supply section.

Directions: Trace and transfer the heart design to stencil paper or manila folder. Cut this out with a craft knife such as X-Acto. Hold the stencil in position on the basket and tap the paint onto the cutout area. Every other heart is red or green and turned right side up or upside down to create an interesting pattern.

You can use this stencil and technique on ornaments, placemats and napkins for a coordinated Christmas decor. The acrylic paint is permanent on fabric and will not come off in the wash. However, it is dissolvable in water when it gets on your hands and the brush can be cleaned in water.

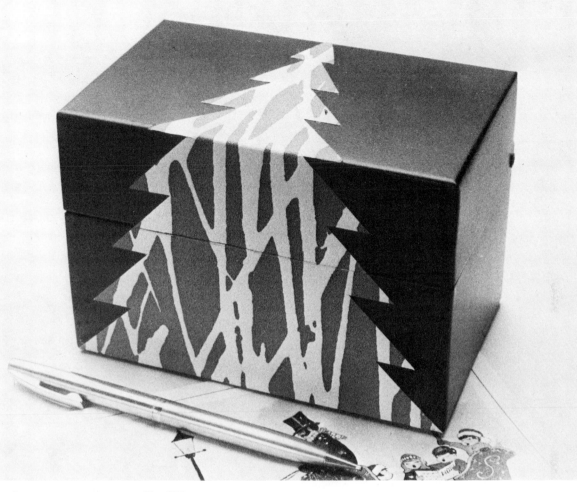

Christmas card file

Keep all the names of those you receive or send Christmas cards to from year to year in a specially made file box. Or give it as a gift to hold favorite Christmas recipes. The metal file box comes in dark green, however I changed the color here to bright red which is optional. These file card boxes can be found in the school and paper supply sections.

Materials: standard file box, red spray paint, green patterned wrapping paper, wallpaper or Con-Tact, tracing paper, pencil, glue, scissors, razor blade, spray varnish (optional).

Directions: If you want to change the color of the file box spray paint it and prop the lid open while drying. The box may need two or three coats to cover the dark green metal.

Trace the Christmas tree pattern which has been planned to fit on a standard size file box. Transfer it to a decorative paper and cut out. If Con-Tact paper is used peel the backing off and apply to the box. However, if you use non-sticky paper spread a thin coat of glue over the back and position the cutout with the top at the very back edge of the lid. Smooth the cutout over the top, down the front over the opening. Press down all edges so they are secure. Remove any excess glue with a damp sponge.

When dry slit opening with a razor blade. For extra protection spray the entire box with clear varnish.

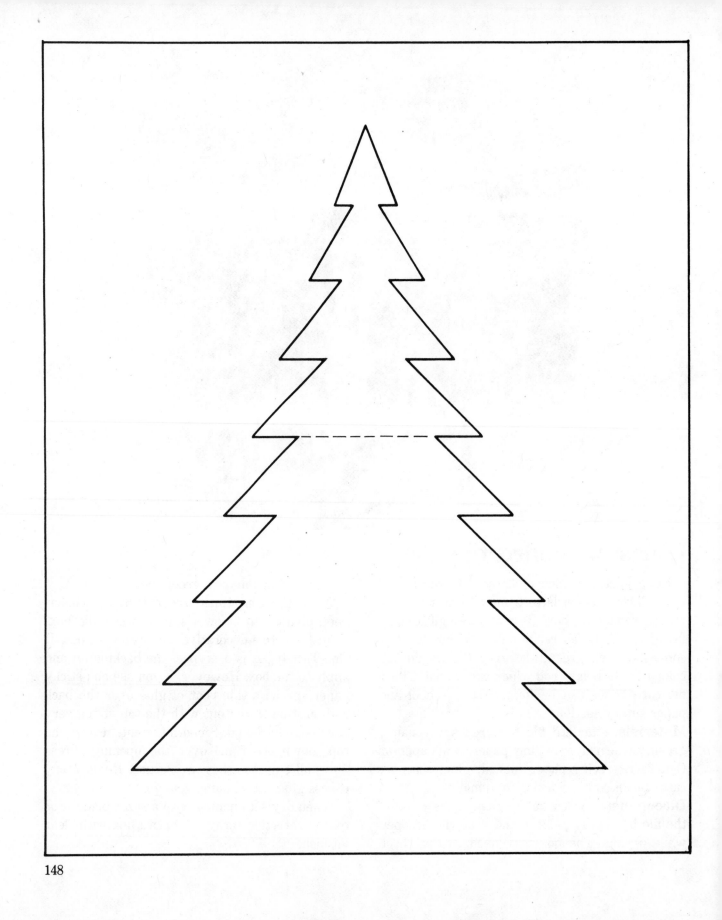

Candy carrier

This is a simple little project that utilizes scraps of material and takes very little time. It's a good way to bring loose candies to someone and they can use the bag again and again. Make bags from red-and-white striped fabric and fill with peppermints or candy canes for Christmas giving.

Materials: 1 piece of fabric 7½ × 15 inches, 2 pieces 2 × 9 inches, 1 yard ½ inch ribbon, needle, thread, scissors.

Directions: Turn each long edge of the large piece under ½ inch and press. Turn 1 inch of the short ends under and press. This piece now measures 7 × 13 inches.

The other pieces will become the handles. Turn long edges under ¼ inch and press. Fold in half lengthwise with wrong sides together. Press and stitch along edges. With 7 × 13 inch piece wrong side up, pin each handle 1½ inches from edges at each short end. Stitch in place. Measure 4 inches in from each short edge and mark with a pin. (See diagram.) Fold the fabric so the handles meet and stitch side seams together stopping at pin marks on either side.

Push the open ends on the bottom up to the inside of the bag. Sew the pointed end of the open piece to the inside side seams. This will hold the bottom closed.

Fill with candy, guest soaps, sewing articles, or cosmetics and tie with the ribbon. This project was designed and made by Ruth Linsley.

Outdoor patio table

The five and ten has expanded to include a variety of household accessories such as inexpensive occasional tables, fold-up chairs, and lamps. You'll be amazed at what you can find that resembles the most expensive version of these familiar items. It's a good place to find well-designed cheap versions of such items as the famous Parson's table. Made of plastic, it's great for outdoor or family-room use. The colors range from bright orange and yellow to the more subdued black, white and chocolate brown used for the next project.

I found the prices ranging from a low of $2.99 in Florida to a high of $5.99 in New York. At the low price it's a steal. At the highest price it's still a bargain. Here are my two versions. Each design was influenced by the area they came from. The orange table design was created by cutting up a plastic souvenir shopping bag.

Materials: 1 plastic Parson's table, paper design to cut from a shopping bag, calendar, wrapping paper or greeting cards, white glue, scissors, damp sponge, spray varnish.

Directions: Cut the illustrations from the background and arrange them on the table. If you want to eliminate the cutting, look for decals that suit the project.

Spread glue on the back of each cutout and pat it in place on the table top. Use the damp sponge to press the cutouts down and wipe away excess glue.

Let this dry for a few minutes. Coat the surface with clear spray varnish, such as Krylon, to protect the design. When dry, spray again. If the table will be used outdoors, a third and fourth coat of varnish is necessary.

Occasional table

Any bold floral cotton print can be used to create this table top design. Look for remnants of material in pastel colors to use against a dark background. The flowers are cut out of the fabric print; however, once given a protective coating of varnish, this table can be used outdoors. (See project on page 64.)

Materials: 1 plastic Parson's table, fabric, sharp scissors, white glue, damp sponge, clear fast-drying spray varnish.

Directions: Cut out each flower, stem, and leaf. It's best to eliminate any delicate areas of the design and concentrate on using the larger elements.

Arrange the cutouts on the table top. Cut away or add more leaves, a bud, or extend a stem where needed. Remove one piece at a time and coat the back with white glue. Replace it on the table and pat down with the damp sponge.

Coat with 3 to 4 applications of spray varnish, allowing each to dry between coats. Even if the table will not be used outdoors, it's a good idea to protect it with the varnish.

Kids' corner

The five and ten is the perfect place to begin when planning a wall of storage for a child's room. You can create a complete area to store everything for under $50. You will always find the best supply in the springtime when people generally clean out and organize their closets. In the best-stocked stores you will find fold-up cardboard dressers in 3 different sizes, the most expensive of which is approximately $15. Also made of sturdy cardboard is a 9 and 12 space unit of open cubby holes to hold shoes, toys, underwear, books, etc. The most familiar item which is carried in all stores is the deep storage box with a lift-off lid. These come in a variety of ample sizes and each has a plastic handle at either end for easy moveability.

The biggest drawback is the look of these items. While serviceable they tend to wind up in the closet or under beds for out-of-the-way storage. However, with very little talent, time, or imagination they can be transformed for good-looking out front furniture.

Materials: cardboard storage boxes in 3 different sizes, 4 drawer cardboard dresser (comes with knobs), plastic wastebasket, leftover wallpaper such as Wall-Tex vinyl pre-pasted wallcovering used here, or Con-Tact paper, scissors, ruler, decorative cutouts from greeting cards or wallcovering such as the Sesame Street characters cut from Wall-Tex wallcovering.

Directions: Measure all sides of the cardboard boxes to be covered and rule off on the paper. Be sure to plan carefully so that the designs match where they meet at the corners. Cut each piece slightly larger than the measure.

If you are using Con-Tact or pre-pasted vinyl no glue is necessary. If you are using paper coat the back of each piece with Elmer's Glue-All before attaching it to the box. Be sure that the designs are lined up properly, especially when using a striped pattern. Smooth each piece of covering over the surface and leave to dry before using. The handles at either end of the boxes can be covered with paper as well.

When covering the dresser, cut each drawer piece large enough to slightly overlap into the top of the drawer and around on either side. When the drawer is pulled open it will look finished on all edges.

Cut one large piece to cover both sides and top and leave a little extra to go under on each side. The covering should fold a little to the back as well as over the front edges. Insert drawer pulls after the entire project is finished.

Add the decorative characters last. To do this cut out the individual illustrations and position on each drawer front. Coat the back of each with white glue (the Sesame St. wallcovering is pre-pasted and can be applied with water) and reapply where planned. The combination of different paper patterns and the individual cutouts will give your child's room a distinctive personality. Select those decorations that have meaning to him or her. The striped and polka-dotted background paper is excellent for this or you can use an overall print and forget about the added cutouts.

To protect the paper surface on all cover-ups give each a coat of clear spray varnish. This is not necessary if vinyl or Con-Tact is used. These materials are excellent for such a project because they can be cleaned with a damp sponge.

No-sew place mat

This place mat was planned for a Fourth of July party and the color scheme is red, white and blue. Make yours any combination of colors you want because the simple no-sew technique for the decoration is seam binding which comes in every color imaginable. It's less expensive than ribbon and easier to work with. The new bindings also come with a self-adhesive backing so all you do is position each band and iron it to the fabric. Follow the diagram and you can't miss.

Materials: Solid fabric 13 × 17 inches for 1 place mat, 1 package of red and 1 package of blue iron-on seam binding (Wm. E. Wright), pins.

Directions: Turn the edges of the fabric under to create a ¼ inch hem all around. Place a strip of navy blue seam binding around the back edge of each side and press with a hot iron. Turn the place mat face up on your ironing board.

Cut 4 pieces of red binding 12 inches long and 4 pieces of blue 12 inches long. Next cut 4 pieces of blue 16 inches long and 4 pieces of red 16 inches long.

Begin by placing 2 red strips together 1 inch from either side. Hold them in place by sticking a pin straight up and down through the seam binding into the ironing board. Press these to the fabric. Next pin 2 strips of red together across the bottom and top of the mat 1 inch from either edge. Leave ½ inch space and run a strip of blue across either end. Place a blue strip at either side of the mat ½ inch from the double strip of red.

Finish off all edges with a band of blue and iron the entire place mat. This project can be thrown in the washing machine and ironed without any difficulty. The seam binding will not come off.

Lacy cross-stitch pillows

Any cotton grid-designed fabric is excellent for cross-stitch projects. The most readily available material found in the five and ten is gingham. It comes in a variety of colors in varying sized checks. The technique of cross-stitch is perhaps the most popular among needleworkers because it is easy to do and the results are always perfect. The size of your finished design will depend on the size of the checks in the fabric. There is no need to transfer a pattern. You simply copy the charted design square by square.

Materials: Enough fabric to cover a 14 inch square pillow (if the fabric is 45 inches wide you will need ½ yard), polyfoam pillow form, white cotton embroidery floss, needle, pins, embroidery hoop, scissors.

Directions: Cut 2 squares of fabric 15 × 15 inches. Allow for a ½ inch seam allowance all around before determining where to start your counted cross-stitch design.

With the front of 1 square up insert the material between the embroidery hoop frame. Be sure to position it to correspond with the

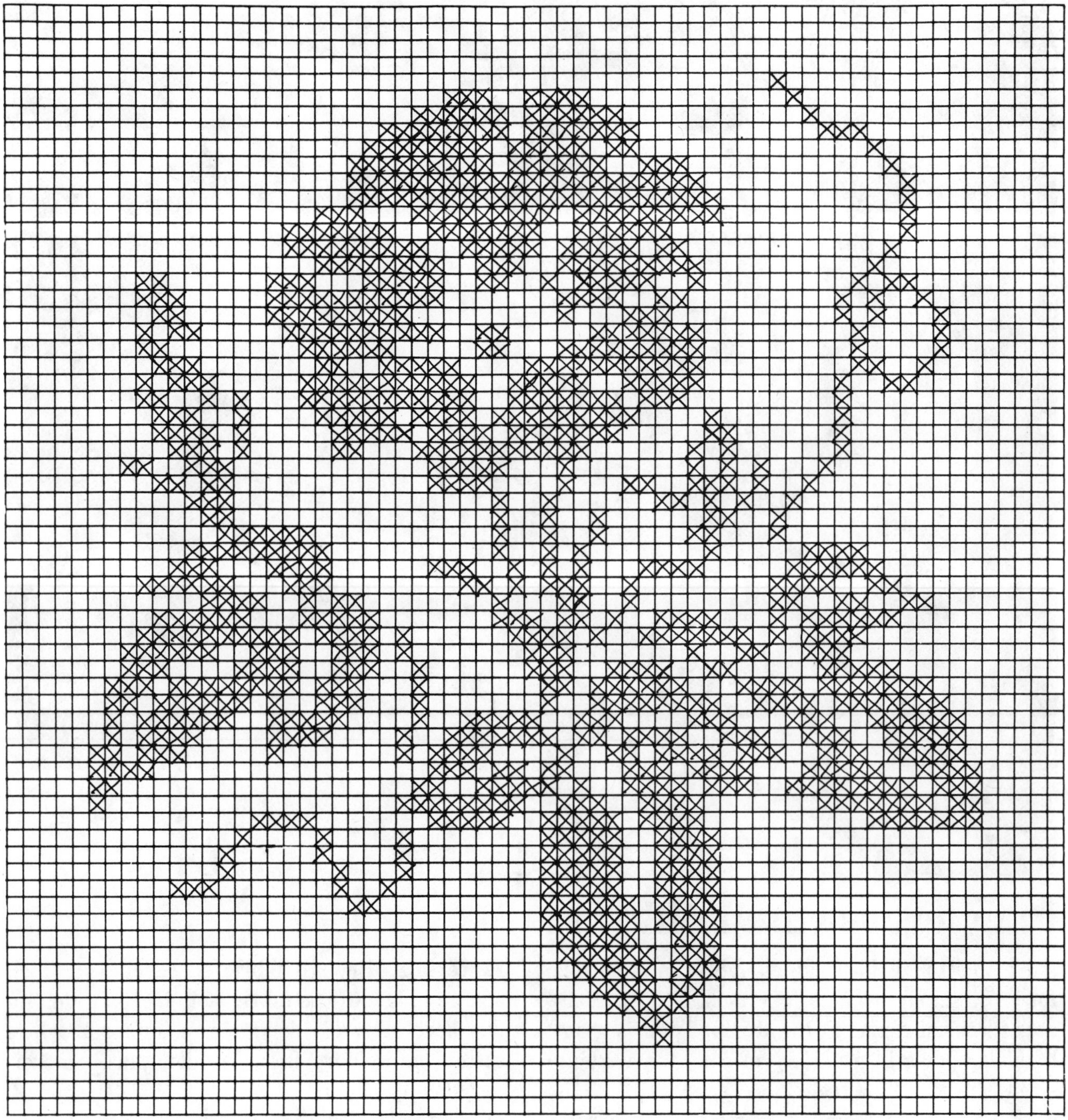

charted design.

Cross-stitch is, as its name implies, an X which, when placed in a series according to a charted pattern, creates a neat, crisp motif. The best way to work it is by stitching all lines slanted in one direction and then the other. All top threads must cross over in the same direction. When completed, this floral design will look like a lacy fillet often found in crochet. Use all white on a red or green background to achieve this as shown here. Or, if you prefer you can use a variety of colors on a light background. The solid color is easier to work and the design is quite strong.

When finished, press from the wrong side. Pin right sides of the 2 pieces of material together. Stitch around 3 sides leaving a ½ inch seam allowance. Trim excess material and cut off the corners. Turn and press from the back. Insert the pillow form. Turn the top edge in and slip stitch the opening or add a zipper.

Picture pretty

A wooden cutting or bread board is a good buy. It's thick and comes in several shapes and sizes. There is a hole drilled in the top for hanging. Thinner and smaller cutting boards called cocktail size, used in home bars, are quite inexpensive. Both provide a good background for mounting photographs. Combined with paper doilies, decals, and cutout paper designs you can create an old-fashioned setting, reminiscent of an elaborate Valentine, for a child's picture or a wedding portrait.

Materials: board, photograph, acrylic paint, brush, varnish (or clear nail polish if the project is small), brush cleaner, doilies, decals, paper cutouts, white glue, scissors.

Directions: The boards are smooth and do not need sanding, so you can begin with a coat of acrylic paint. One board is white, the smaller one pink with a brown trim.

Trim the photograph if necessary and glue it to the center of the board. For the larger project I cut strips of blue wrapping paper to create a ribbon band around the photo edges. The large rose in the right-hand corner is a decal. All the other elements were cut from wrapping paper, including the little bow at the top. Arrange the designs around and overlapping the edges of your photograph and glue them to the board.

For the smaller project the center of a small doily is cut away and the remaining portion is glued over the photograph to create a round frame. Pieces of a gold doily are cut and glued around the edges of the board and cut-out flowers and bow are then added over all.

To create a smooth and protective finish, varnish is applied either from a can or spray. Three or 4 coats should be applied for complete coverage. If you don't want to be bothered with the varnish, float clear nail polish over the surface and leave undisturbed while drying.

To hang the breadboard, a small blue ribbon is tied through the hole. To hang the smaller frame you will have to add a small picture-hanging tab (hardware) on the back.

Sources for supplies

All materials used in this book were purchased in a 5 and 10 cent store. If you cannot find a product in your area for making any of the projects, or if you would like to obtain full-size patterns for craft projects, write to:

Leslie Linsley Enterprises
Main Street
Nantucket, Mass 02554